SNCF

David Haydock

MODERN RAILWAYS SPECIAL

LONDON
IAN ALLAN LTD

First published 1991

ISBN 0 7110 1980 0

All rights reserved. No part of this book may be reproduced or transmitted in any form or by any means, electronic or mechanical, including photocopying, recording or by any information storage and retrieval system, without permission from the Publisher in writing.

© D. Haydock 1991

Published by Ian Allan Ltd, Shepperton, Surrey; and printed by Ian Allan Printing Ltd at their works at Coombelands in Runnymede, England

Design and Artwork by R. Wilcockson

Front: **TGV-Atlantique.** *SNCF*

Back cover top: **A two-car DMU in Pays de la Loire Region Livery.** *SNCF*

Back cover bottom: **A TGV-Sud-Est set near Paris passes a double-deck EMU set on a suburban service.** *SNCF*

Below: **During May 1991, SNCF prototype No BB 10003 was tested in Belgium - seen here at Tournai. The locomotive is used as a test-bed for traction motors and electrical equipment destined for Channel Tunnel 'TMST' high-speed trains.** *Rail Info Collection*

Contents

Introduction	3
A Brief History of French Railways	4
SNCF Today	5
Passenger Services	9
TGV	13
Regional Passenger Services	22
Paris	31
Freight	37
The Human Factor	45

Introduction

Describing any organisation like French National Railways — *Société Nationale des Chemins de Fer Français* (SNCF) at one particular moment is not unlike trying to photograph a butterfly flitting from flower to flower. However, the SNCF does work to a five-year plan, the latest of which covers 1990-1994 and which forms the basis for much of this book. A book based entirely on a dry-as-dust corporate plan would certainly not make much of a read. Having lived in France for eight years, and in that time having met a multitude of railwaymen within this behemoth, I hope that I am in a good position to interpret its development, particularly from an Englishman's point of view.

The French magazine *Le Nouvel Economiste* carried an article recently entitled 'SNCF goes off the rails'. This was not a critical piece claiming French Railways had lost their way, but pertained to SNCF's increasing resort to road transport to replace or complement its rail services. I believe that it may not be long before SNCF may have to change its name to something akin to SFT — *Société Française des Transports* — transport in the plural as SNCF is increasingly managed as a multi-modal group, albeit with a rail core. This core is tending to stay the same size whilst the activities of the 293 group subsidiaries are continually growing in importance, accounting for 26% of group turnover in 1990 against 19% in 1985. Both externally and internally, SNCF management are at pains to stress the synergy both past and future within the group. This can be a difficult message to impress on the rail lobby when passenger or freight services are transferred to road, as is common at present.

SNCF is known to British transport enthusiasts and professionals principally as purveyor of high speed, thanks to the enormous success, both technically and financially, of the *Train à Grande Vitesse* (TGV). The development of the TGV is not surprising on a railway so dominated by technocrats. It is they who have made SNCF a network efficient in terms of staff and energy, although perhaps not always in terms of rolling stock. However, technocratic projects are not always the best for the customer, be he a passenger or a freight client. Electrification of a line has been chosen in the past over improvement of rolling stock, bringing scant improvement for the passenger. The technocrats are also weak on marketing, and prefer to reduce service levels rather than try to fill half-empty trains with special offers.

Despite this, the French public has a very favourable perception of SNCF, and considers that the network reflects French modernity. SNCF is also broadly approved of by politicians across the spectrum and therefore the national railways are not the whipping boy they often represent in Britain. As a nationalised industry, SNCF is closely controlled by government, which some may consider a disadvantage. However, when it is a government which is convinced of the importance of a good rail network and one which is willing to back the railway operator and its development projects, such a drawback pales somewhat.

The future for SNCF is spelt TGV, and is probably rosy, although costs are rising. But what of the other SNCF services? Paris suburban services, which are already equal to the best in the world, will continue to expand and interconnect, particularly within the Regional Express Network. Further projects are in the pipeline for the modernisation of passenger services in the French provinces, but there is some way to go yet. Freight services certainly 'could do better', and it remains to be seen whether present comprehensive reshaping will pay off. Most preoccupying for me is the fate of middle-distance passenger services, which are poor and getting worse. Will the TGV age bring their dismantlement?

In this *Modern Railways Special* I will describe all these developments. But also I shall pay tribute to SNCF drivers, although I mean them to represent the workforce as a whole — a team of professionals, passionately committed to railways and their efficient operation.

Acknowledgements

I would like to thank the following people who have helped me research this book: Jacques Fournier, President of SNCF, Jean-Didier Bodin, Lille Regional Director, and many other SNCF managers and staff including Alain de Teissière, Pierre Tamba, Jean Corseaux, Alfred Fabian, Maurice Testu, Messrs Sauvage, Guerbe, Grenier, Haquette, Legrand, Boktaels plus Mme Gence. Others to thank include M. Fouchet of the Bretagne Region, Nicolas Douez, Bernard Collardey, Jerome Koch, Brian Perren and the staff of *'La Vie du Rail*. Apart from SNCF and UIC reports, I have consulted the magazine *La Vie du Rail* widely, as well as several books including *La Géographie des Transports et du Tourisme.*

Left: **From 1975 until 1987 a much more modern logo was carried. Four years after the introduction of the new logo No 22212 prepares to depart from Nice Ville station.** *John C. Baker*

A Brief History of French Railways

The first railway in France was an 18km line from St Etienne to Andrézieux, opened in July 1827 to carry coal, and was followed swiftly by other lines throughout France. As early as 1842, a law was passed concerning lines to be built into Paris, which gave the State, and therefore the taxpayer, responsibility for the infrastructure — land acquisition and construction of the trackbed — whilst private companies would lay the track, buy the rolling stock and operate the lines. In 1851, 33 such companies existed but eight years later these had been merged into only six — the Nord, Est, Ouest, Orléans, Midi and Paris-Lyon-Méditérranée (PLM).

By 1870 the network was almost complete, and by the beginning of World War 1 France was served by 39,400km of railway. However, many lines were completely unprofitable, and with the war the finances of the companies deteriorated significantly. Already in 1875, France had created a State-owned operating company, the Etat, which bought up 2,800km of bankrupt lines in the following eight years. The Etat system grew gradually to cover most of the west of France plus the former Alsace-Lorraine, recovered from Germany after the war. With further mergers, only five other companies remained in 1937: the Est, Nord, Midi, Paris-Orléans (PO) and PLM. By this time, the companies were for the most part no longer in competition and, indeed, needed to work in consort to reduce expenses and develop the system as a whole. A fusion of networks thus took place on 1 January 1938 with the creation of the SNCF, a semi-public company in which the State owned 51% of the capital, the rest remaining with the old private companies. The statute of the SNCF gave it the management of the rail network for a period of 45 years, which ended on 31 December 1982. In exchange, SNCF had a common carrier duty and levied fares subject to government approval.

The immediate history of the SNCF after creation was linked to World War 2, in which severe damage was sustained due to enemy and allied bombardments. Reconstruction followed, and then began a period of modernisation, which in most cases came with electrification. It was in the 1950s that SNCF adopted industrial alternating current at 25kV as standard, although there existed a significant kilometrage of track already electrified at 1,500V dc south of Paris, which meant that major new dc projects continued into the 1960s. By this time SNCF had developed dual-voltage locomotives, and further dc electrification has since only been carried out for local operating convenience.

SNCF gained a reputation for high-speed developments after the 1955 record when two electric locomotives reached 331km/h on the Bordeaux-Hendaye line. Regular high speed operation gradually reached 160km/h, then 200km/h with line upgrading, and particularly with the introduction of modern electric classes in the 1960s and gas turbine trains in 1972. Out of the gas turbines came the TGV, which became an electric design partly because of the 1973 oil shock. Finally introduced on a completely new line in 1981, the TGV is now the major instrument of rail development in France.

Little changed in the status of SNCF until 1971, when the government introduced a duty to break even after subsidy. However, this feat was rarely actually achieved, and losses were added to SNCF's growing debt. At the end of 1982, the 45-year statute governing the SNCF came to an end and a new transport law known as LOTI (*Loi d'orientation des transports intérieurs* — law on internal transport policy) set out the future status of the SNCF as well as all other forms of land transport in France. SNCF became a 'public establishment of an industrial and commercial character'. In September 1983 the French government set out the new relationship between itself and the SNCF and, in particular, the principles of SNCF's financial relationship with central and local, especially regional, government.

The LOTI has been the base of a significant metamorphosis of French railways over the last eight years due to its redefinition of the role of the SNCF. But LOTI also arrived at a time of worst-ever results for SNCF. Despite subsidies, SNCF registered a loss of over 8 billion francs in 1983. Since this year, SNCF has steadily improved its performance and, in 1990, accounts were almost exactly balanced. The major preoccupation in 1990 is the *Société* debt, cumulated during the years of high losses, and which now weighs heavily in overall finances. The 1990-1994 *Contrat de Plan*, which defines relations with government, specifies that SNCF will receive no State support apart from agreed subsidies. These subsidies, however, now include substantial yearly sums to help SNCF pay off its debt which is expected to be eliminated by the year 2002.

Since LOTI, one can say that SNCF has gradually evolved into more distinct 'sectors' of activity, although not by specific design as in the case of British Rail. Passenger services are now divided into 'Intercités' (intercity services) which, in principle, cover all their costs, 'regional' services which are supported financially under agreements with the 22 regional councils, and Paris suburban services which are heavily subsidised. Freight and parcels (SNCF subsidiary SERNAM) are the remaining two sectors of activity.

Another aspect to be stressed is the emergence of SNCF as a multi-modal transport group dominated by rail activity. For many years, SNCF has created or bought subsidiaries such as Servirail (catering), SGW (wagon hiring), CNC (container services) and Cariane (coach and bus services). Only now does SNCF seem to be reaping the full benefits of group synergy in the creation of new logistical services.

At the end of 1989 SNCF operated over a network of 30,909km, of which 12,430km was electrified and 10,440km was freight only. In 1990 the network carried 842 million passengers (64 billion passenger kilometres) of which 530 million travelled on the Paris suburban network. Altogether, 142.4 million tonnes of freight (51.5 billion tonne km) were hauled, 202,083 staff were employed by SNCF in 1990, and turnover was FF74.4 billion (£7.44 billion).

SNCF Today

Despite the change in the statute of SNCF which took place in 1983, its relationship with the State is virtually unchanged. Central government owns almost all SNCF's capital, and controls the SNCF board closely through the appointment of senior civil servants, who occupy 10 of the 18 seats on the board. The President is also appointed by the government of the day and, if required, is sacked or forced to resign — SNCF had four different Presidents between 1986 and 1989, due to a succession of crises, particularly regarding safety.

A contract, the *Contrat de Plan*, sets out the statutory relationship between SNCF and government and is renewed every five years. This sets out SNCF's strategic objectives, some of which are overtly political, such as *aménagement du territoire* — national strategic planning. Although this sort of objective could be seen as a handicap, it also means that the government is tied into such projects as the construction of TGV lines, in the same way as it is committed to motorway building. Thus, SNCF has the implicit government support which was so lacking for the Channel Tunnel Rail Link through Kent. As the contract also stipulates streamlining of the freight business, the government is also, by inference, supporting SNCF management rather than the trade unions, where job losses are necessary. However, another part of the contract lays on SNCF a responsibility to 'improve the working conditions of railwaymen' and to 'modernise the pay structure' which, of course, will be taken whichever way management or unions prefer to interpret it.

The contract also sets out limits on passenger fares increases (although freight rates are completely uncontrolled). For the moment, this is limited to the general level of inflation (the Minister of Finance keeping a close eye on the prices index in which SNCF fares weigh heavily) and based loosely on the distance travelled. However, the State now gives SNCF complete liberty to vary increases within this limit. SNCF has used this freedom to reduce long distance fares where air competition is strong, and increase revenue on TGV services with its RESA range of supplements, a policy which is set to spread to most intercity services. The problems that such restrictions on pricing cause are clear — SNCF has no way of recovering abnormal increases in costs. For the rail unions, the message is the same — it is impossible to increase salaries above the rate of inflation

Organigramme of SNCF top management structure (revised 1990)

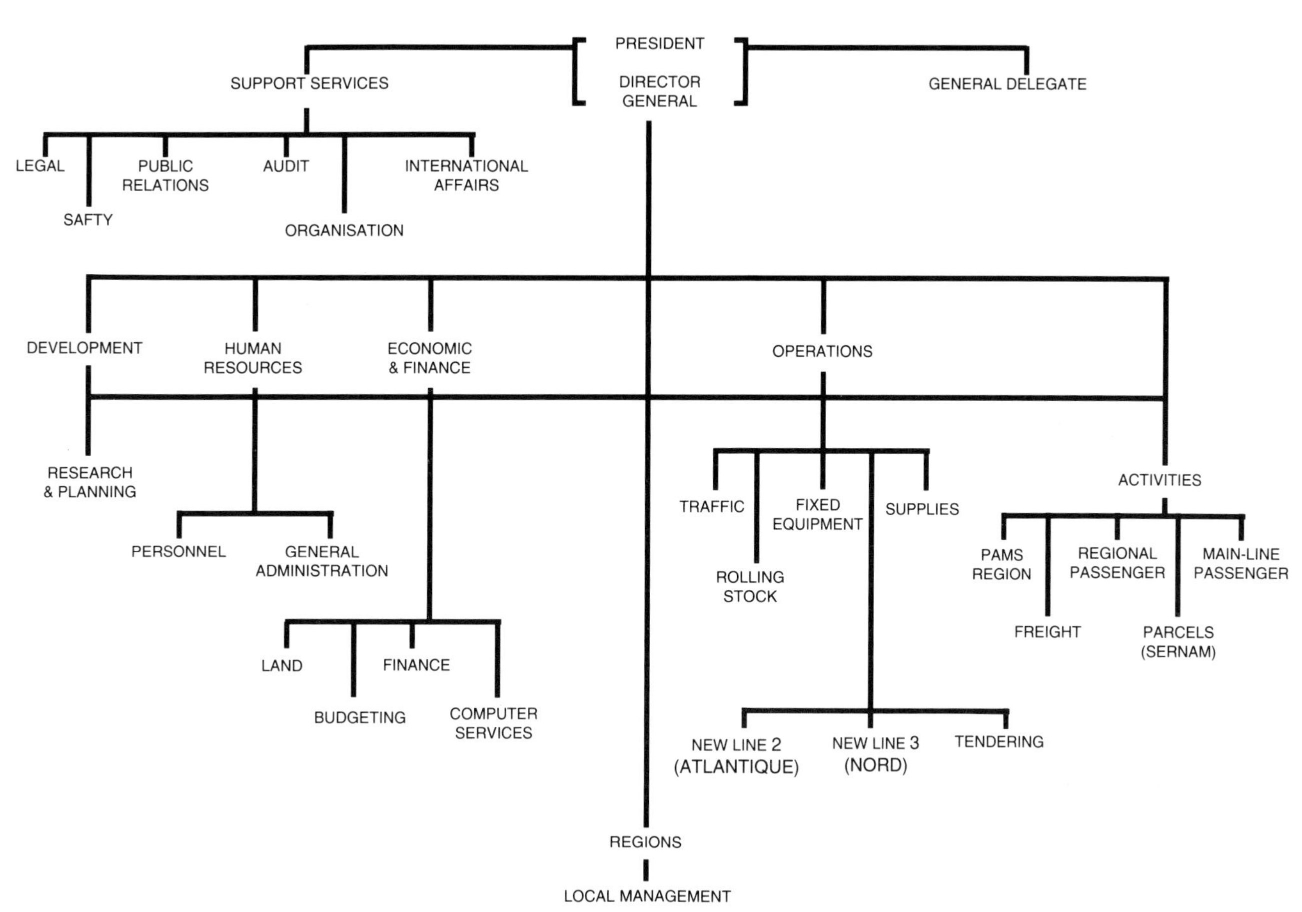

SNCF Results 1984-89						
	1984	1985	1986	1987	1988	1989
Direct Rail Receipts	35,713*	37,966*	37,171*	37,242	38,793	40,460
Fares Compensations	5,330*	5,690*	5,550*	5,575	5,644	6,000*
Total Rail Receipts	41,043	43,656	42,721	42,817	44,437	46,460
Debt elimination	3,510	3,250	3,000	3,542	3,853	4,019
Regional Services	3,060	2,949	3,313	3,463	3,508	3,671
Paris Suburban	1,144	1,100	998	1,045	947	1,018
Infrastructure	10,103	10,642	11,000	11,367	10,029	10,382
Others	45	14	34	18	142	150*
Total Subsidies	23,192*	23,645*	23,895*	25,010	24,123	25,240*
*estimated						
Source: SNCF Annual Reports All values in FF 1,000s						

without economies elsewhere.

On the other hand, the State-SNCF contract stipulates the central government contributions to SNCF coffers and the reasons for them. SNCF's accounts for 1984-1989 are shown above.

The table above shows that direct receipts from SNCF rail services reached over FF 40 billion (£4 billion) in 1989. The contribution from other subsidiaries of the SNCF group considerably increase this total. State contributions amounted to around FF 25 billion. Not included are the considerable State contribution to SNCF pensions, and further sums from the French regional councils.

The largest State contribution is that to SNCF's infrastructure costs (around FF 10 billion a year), with the aim of 'harmonising the conditions of competition of the various modes of transport'. In principle this compensates for competing amounts going into the road system, airports and canals. Not included in the table is the State's considerable contribution to SNCF's pension fund of around FF 14 billion per year, equivalent to 27% of the normal employer's contribution plus 9% of the employees contribution.

Contributions are also given in exchange for SNCF's public service role — an unspecified amount compensates for lines and installations necessary for the country's defence and more public contributions are transferred for regional services (FF 3.7 billion), Paris suburban services (the *indemnité compensatrice banlieue* worth FF 1 billion in 1989) and to compensate for the granting of price reductions to certain 'social' categories such as invalids, large families and old people. This amounted to FF 6 billion in 1989, of which FF 2.3 billion was for the Paris suburbs — more than the direct receipts in this region. Finally, a special 'temporary' contribution, totalling FF 4 billion in 1989 is destined to help SNCF write off its debt, which totalled FF 100 billion in 1988. Prior to 1989 a similar amount was allocated to help SNCF restructure in order to reduce long term costs.

Although never far from the limelight, SNCF is not the political whipping horse that British Rail represents in Britain. In their great majority, the French public, politicians and decision-makers have confidence in SNCF, and continue to use its services. None of the political parties believes that privatisation of SNCF would be a good thing. And so long as SNCF presents the country with products and records which make France a rail shop window, the heat would seem to be off.

SNCF finds itself under political pressure from many sides over its policies of job shedding, line and station closures, service reductions, etc. Government attitudes are now very different from those in the early 1980s, when the Socialists obliged SNCF to take on workers and reopen lines at a time of declining traffic. Certainly, the political clout of the more than 200,000 *cheminots* (railwaymen) is not negligible. This élite, dominated by the communist-led trade union CGT, which jealously guard their 'acquisitions', such as retirement at 55(50 for drivers), have made more than a few ministers tremble in their boots. Since the seven-week strike which left people stranded in the freezing winter of 1986/87, SNCF management and government alike have regularly stressed the 'social progress' taking place in the enterprise, and have allocated considerable sums to improving the railwayman's lot.

Traffic and Financial Results
SNCF turned in a small 'profit' in 1990.

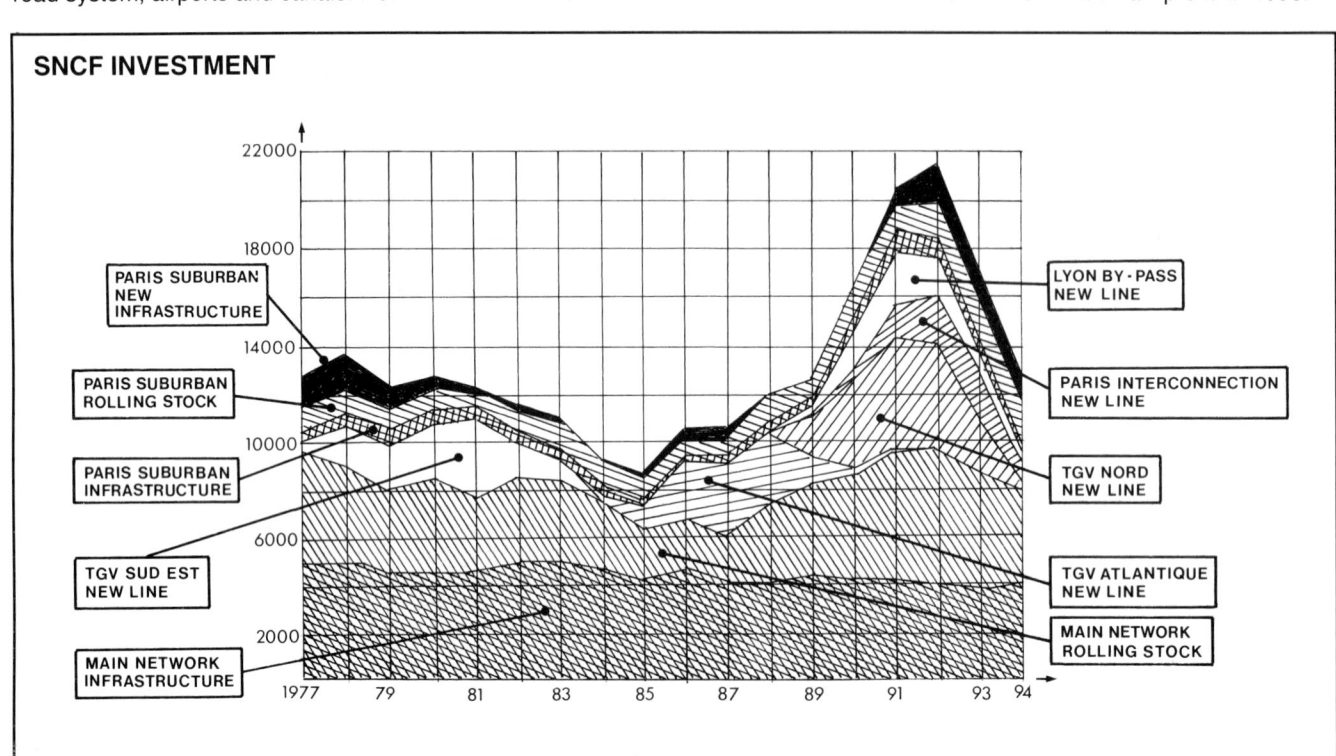

SNCF Receipts 1984-1990

	1984	1985	1986	1987	1988	1989	1990	Change
Main line passenger	17,704	19,682	19,486	20,046	21,604	23,024	24,279	+37%
Paris suburban	3,872	4,177	4,377	4,550	4,766	5,010	5,470	+41%
Freight	15,230	15,493	14,565	14,115	13,868	14,094	13,574	-11%
Sernam (Parcels)	3,569	3,664	3,681	3,491	3,573	3,716	3,946	+10%

(million FF)

SNCF Traffic 1984-1990

	1984	1985	1986	1987	1988	1989	1990	Change
Passengers(millions)								
Main line	290	301	297	300	311	314	312	+8%
of which TGV	—	15.4	15.6	17.0	18.1	20.7	29.9	+94%
Paris Suburban	—	465	475	482	499	511	530	+14%
Total Passenger km (billions)	60.2	62.1	59.9	60.0	63.3	64.5	63.95	+6%
Freight								
Tonne (millions)	177	162	146	142	145	147	142	-20%
Tonne km(billions)	58.4	55.8	51.7	51.3	52.3	53.3	51.5	-12%

COMPARISON OF EUROPEAN RAIL NETWORKS

	Network Length km	Of Which Electrified km	Passengers Staff	Passenger Carried Millions	Tonnes km	Freight	Tonne km
BR	16,599	4,382	149,900	763.7	34,315	149.5	18,104
DB	27,278	11,669	251,344	1,025.9	40,959	273.9	58,972
FS	16,015	9,311	214,298	410.0	43,343	58.0	19,663
RENFE	12,531	6,315	52,961	194.2	15,716	28.5	11,403
SNCF	34,365	12,008	213,214	801.1	63,057	143.3	51,527

Source: UIC Statistics, 1988

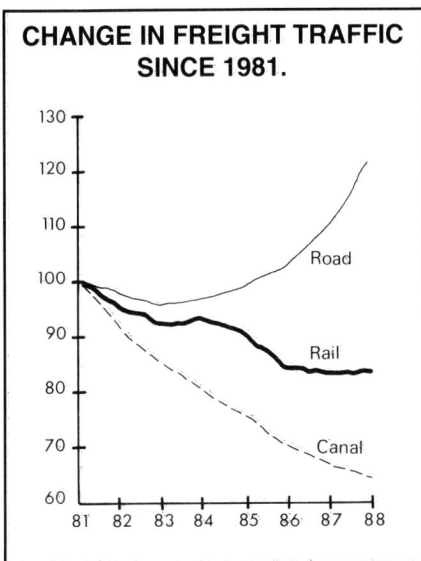

CHANGE IN FREIGHT TRAFFIC SINCE 1981.

This of course takes into account all contributions from the State, but represents a real turnround for SNCF's finances. In 1983 the *Société Nationale* posted a worst-ever loss of FF 8.84 billion, even after these same contributions. Action taken by management since has brought a dangerous slide into the mire under strict control. Of course the action necessary has not been without pain, and staff numbers have taken the brunt of the attack on costs, falling from 251,000 in 1983 to 202,000 in 1990. A small number of lines have been closed to passengers and other services have been partially or entirely transferred to bus. Far more have been closed to freight, the FERCAM lorry service taking over (see chapter on freight services).

Whatever recovery there has been is more attributable to cost reductions than to increases in revenue. Growth in passenger traffic has averaged 1-2% per year and passenger revenue over the period 1984-1989 (see above) has been firm. However, this has done little more than keep pace with inflation in real terms, despite the major contribution from growth in TGV traffic. On the other hand, freight traffic and revenue have followed a constant downward trend, only bucked in 1989, and unfortunately continuing in 1990 due to recessionary pressures.

Productivity

Although comparisons are renowned for being odious, it is impossible to place SNCF without some cross-references to British Rail and other principal European rail networks (omitting Belgium and The Netherlands as they are small and urban, and Switzerland and Austria because of their size and terrain).

At over 34,000km, SNCF has the longest rail network in Europe, not including the reunified Germany which at the time of writing has yet genuinely to reunite its railways. On this network, SNCF carries fewer passengers than German Federal Railways (DB) and not many more than BR. However, each passenger travels much further (79km on average) than in West Germany (40km) and Britain (45km), thus making French passenger km the highest in Europe.

SNCF also carries far fewer tonnes of freight than DB (former Eastern Bloc countries also greatly exceed SNCF's total), and even BR, with its myriad short heavy hauls of coal, carries more tonnes than SNCF. Once again, each tonne of freight travels much further, so that in terms of tonne km, SNCF is almost on a par with DB.

It should be stressed that, although SNCF receives large subsidies from government, its financial situation is vastly better than that of DB, which sinks further into the deficitory mire each year. Italian Railways (FS) are also very profligate in comparison with SNCF — with approximately the same staff numbers, FS hauls 31% fewer passenger km and 62% fewer tonne km of freight! Taking a facile measure of productivity — comparing staff employed with the number of passenger km plus tonne km carried, SNCF shows itself to be the most efficiently run network of the five considered here.

SNCF does not publish many statistics on productivity as such, preferring to be judged simply by the number of passenger km and freight km hauled, without reference to the resources mobilised to do so. However, it is clear from the aforegoing statistics that productivity has increased considerably in the 1980s as revenue held firm whilst staff numbers diminished considerably.

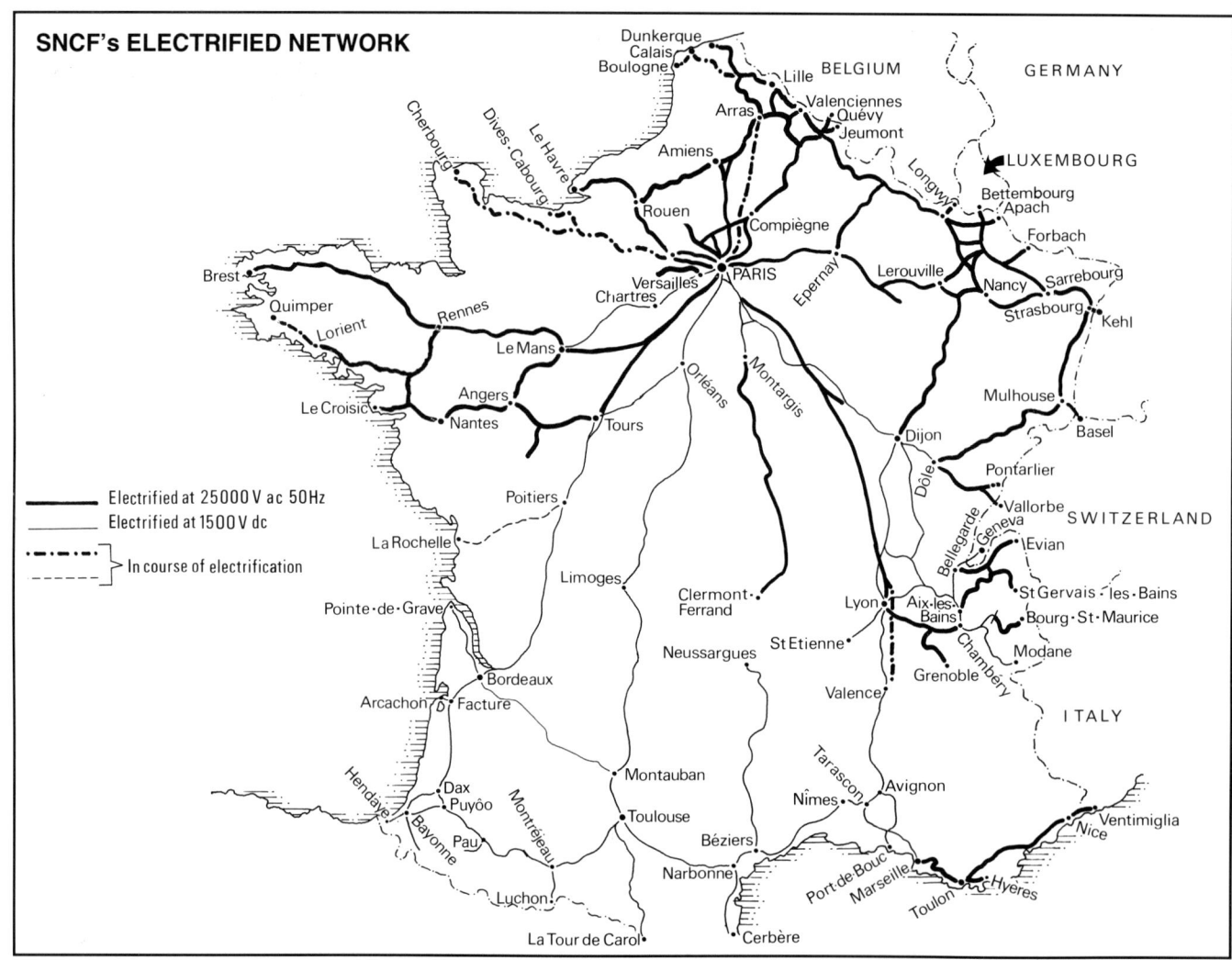

Principal productivity statistics are on the 'equivalent kilometric units' (a method of expressing passenger and freight traffic together) per member of staff. Since 1983, this has risen by 28% from 562,000 to 717,000. Figures for rolling stock productivity have not been published since the mid-1980s but rough calculations from what figures are available suggest that only small gains have been made in recent years. The really remarkable improvements have been in maintenance periods, particularly for electric locomotives. Since 1974 the average period between overhauls has risen from 600,000km to 1,040,000km, a gain of 73%. This performance was possible due to the excellent Alsthom designs of the 1970s. Strasbourg-based BB15000 Bo-Bo 25kV electrics built 1971-78 are renowned for travelling up to 3 million km between overhauls!

Investment
The 1990-1994 plan stipulates that 34% of investment should be self-financed, and sets out the other sources possible. In most cases, there are two other sources — central government itself and local government, in most cases the Regions. This is the case for projects such as electrification and station improvements, although for TGV different rules apply. The Contract also states that if the state, local government or a public organisation demands a change to an SNCF investment plan, they must put in money so that there is no adverse effect on SNCF finances. This stipulation, which was first introduced in 1985, has been used to good effect in some intricate negotiations by SNCF. Thus, the electrification of Poitiers-La Rochelle, which will allow the TGV-Atlantique to reach the Atlantic coast, was possible through contributions from nine different sources, including town councils and chambers of commerce.

Although allowed to borrow money in the international money markets to finance investment, SNCF is not totally free concerning its financial dealings, and the Finance Ministry has in the past forced SNCF to resort to currency borrowings which were not as financially advantageous as other options.

The organisation of SNCF management is still very production based, with operations parallel rather than subservient to what we might consider the 'sector' managers. Indeed, management by activity (market sector) was introduced only during 1990 when the managers of the intercity, regional passenger, Paris suburban, freight and parcels sectors were promoted to positions in which they report direct to SNCF President, (see Organigramme). Whether they will ever obtain the power over the engineers and operators which BR sector leaders now have remains to be seen. Certainly, the freight manager, Alain Poinssot, cast a jealous eye across the Channel recently when scarce locomotives were allocated to hopelessly loss-making passenger services, leaving his potentially profitable freight trains to run late. Some 'Regionalisation' is occuring, however with responsibility for regional passenger services recently transferred to area managers, under the wing of 'regional actions' director.

Given the very close links with government, the reader will not be surprised to learn that SNCF high-flyers are more civil servants than commercial managers. Recruited almost exclusively from the most prestigious engineering schools, they have favoured progress led by technical development over market-led initiatives. In the case of the TGV, a superb technical achievement coincided with the desire for speed felt by a large chunk of the passenger market. However, the success of the TGV is now masking the paucity of ideas to capture other markets.

Passenger Services

At 30,909km, the SNCF network is the longest in Europe but is one of the least dense, reflecting France's large area and low population density of around 100 people/km sq — Great Britain is around 300/km sq and the area south of a Mersey-Tyne line is even denser. The mountainous areas of France — the Alps, Pyrenees and Massif Central — and a large band to the east of Paris have densities of 20 people or less.

In 1990, the network carried 825 million passengers (64 billion passenger kilometres), of which 530 million travelled on the Paris suburban network. The network is highly centralised on Paris, and despite relatively successful attempts to promote the provincial Regions, this centralisation is being repeated with the construction of the TGV network. The Ile-de-France region around Paris accounts for around 10 million souls, or nearly one fifth of the French total. No other conurbation approaches this total — only five other agglomerations exceed half a million inhabitants: Marseille (1,716,000), Lyon (1,240,000), Lille (946,000), Bordeaux (650,000) and Toulouse (550,000). Other principal urban areas include Rouen (400,000) and Nantes (460,000) plus the regions of Nord-Pas de Calais (4 million), Lorraine (2.3 million) and Alsace (1.6 million). By contrast, the Lozère *département* has only 74,294 inhabitants spread over 5,167sq km. All this means that France cannot support the sort of regular interval timetable found elsewhere in Europe, except in a small number of areas.

To understand how people move around, it is useful to look at how SNCF organises its timetabling and motive power diagrams. Tuesday to Thursday are treated 'basic working days' with a base service. Friday sees many students, soldiers on leave and workers heading home, which often triples base service traffic and creates the need for many reliefs. Saturday, which is a school day in the morning, sees a continuation of this traffic up to around 15.00, followed by a lull until the same time on Sunday, when the exodus starts again in reverse. Monday morning is very busy, but traffic is back to its base by lunchtime.

Important influences on movements include the French education system which 'exiles' teachers to unpopular regions, students who invariably choose to study within a one to two hour train ride of home, returning for the weekend, plus the large number of people who have a flat in town with a house in the country. On the other hand, off-peak travel is quite low. Relatively few people use the train to go shopping, partly due to the dominance of retailing by hypermarkets, and 'tourism' by train at the weekend is rare.

The overall market for personal transport is in continual increase, particularly in the 'visiting friends and relations', tourism and professional categories. However, competition is very strong. The rural nature of France means that a car is essential to most people. 75% of French families own a car and 22% own two cars — these figures were 65 and 13 in 1977. Congestion is still minor in all but the largest towns and parking is usually possible if not often legal. The typical Frenchman still seems so attached to his car that a 15 minute search for a space is no disincentive. France has an

Above left: **The 10 members of Class CC 40100 are the longest locomotives in service with SNCF. Originally equipped to operate over the four different voltages of France (1,500V dc; 25kV ac), Belgium (3,000V dc) and Germany (15kV ac), the Class is used on international services from Paris to Brussels and Liege. No CC 40109 with 12 coaches is seen between Orry-le-Ville and Survilliers with the Amsterdam-Paris 'Etoile du Nord' TEE (now 'Eurocity') service.** *Y. Broncard*

Left: **The Paris-Toulouse route has lost traffic to air services in recent years as the six hour journey time has proved difficult to reduce. The future of the route lies with TGV services via Bordeaux. Photographed in July 1987, No BB 7333 is seen at Gourdon with the 'Ventadour' Paris-Toulouse service.** *Rail Info Collection*

extensive and still expanding motorway system which in most cases is free-flowing. The network counted 6,800km at the beginning of 1989 and will be extended by 4,000km by the end of the century. However, tolls on most sections mean that for drivers travelling alone, rail can be a cheap alternative.

Coaches account for only 6% of the market in France, having been excluded by law from long distance stage carriage work so far. With the abolition of this restrictive law made necessary by EC regulations, it is certain that SNCF's rail services will find themselves under attack on many fronts. As the 1990s began, major manoeuvres were taking place within the French coach and bus industry in order to take advantage of the opportunities presented by liberalisation. A twist in the tail of this problem is that the SNCF group includes some of the major French coach companies. These are not likely to start competing with rail, although in the long term some conflict of interest may occur. At present, the accent is on developing complementary services — coaches connecting into rail in cases where a link did not previously exist. An example is the successful coach feeder from Roanne to Le Creusot TGV station, introduced in 1988.

The long distances between French conurbations mean that driving can be very arduous, and air travel becomes the main rail alternative. Although expense is virtually no object for the businessman, high fares can be a real disincentive to the optional traveller and rail is relatively cheaper. However, air competition has become a real challenge on certain routes, such as Paris-Toulouse, where SNCF has not been able to reduce journey times. Air traffic has grown by 300-500% on many routes in the last 15 years whilst SNCF traffic has stagnated. Only on routes where TGV has been introduced has SNCF traffic grown at an honourable rate.

SNCF divides its passenger services into three categories:

- Intercity
- Regional
- Ile de France (Paris suburban).

Regional and Paris suburban services will be covered in further chapters.

Intercity covers TGV and EuroCity international trains, plus all Rapides and Expresses on principal routes. Most are TGVs or formed of hauled stock, the majority of which is Corail or other high quality air-conditioned stock. Trains of other stock are brought in mainly at peak times of the week and year.

Intercity services generated 47.8 billion passenger km in 1988 and revenue of around FF 19 billion including State contributions for reduced 'social' fares. According to the SNCF five-year plan, after direct costs have been deducted, this gives a net contribution of FF 3 billion. The Intercity category also covers trains on other, less important, lines. An Express can thus be a train on a minor line which is deemed important in completing the Intercity network. For example, the Bordeaux-Bergerac service has one out of its nine trains a day classified as Express, whereas two Expresses operate daily in the opposite direction. These trains are operated with exactly the same stock (DMUs) as the rest of the daily service. Thus, certain trains are sponsored by the Intercity 'sector' and, in principle, should cover their costs. However, on such lines this is rarely the case and these trains are cross-subsidised by main line services, especially TGV.

In the past 10 years, traffic on conventional Intercity services has been stagnant and on many routes continually eroded by improvements to air services and road networks. Since 1972, for example, SNCF traffic between Paris and the west and southwest of France has risen by barely 20% (and was falling until the introduction of TGV-A), whereas air traffic has gone up by 500% on Paris-Toulouse, 400% on Paris-Bordeaux and 350% on Paris-Nantes. Clearly, these figures represent a failure by SNCF to tap a growing market for travel. SNCF is now placing all its bets on TGV, which is set to take an increasing share of the rapidly growing Intercity traffic. At present, TGV represents around 22% of the Intercity total but by 1995, with the opening of the Channel Tunnel, TGV-Nord, Paris and Lyon by-pass lines, this proportion is set to reach well over 50%.

The Development of Intercity Services
On its creation, SNCF inherited a motley selection of rolling stock and services. World War 2 severely damaged the network and interrupted development,

Above left: **Work on the TGV-Nord line from Paris to Lille and the Channel Tunnel was well advanced in 1991, with track laying starting in September of that year. For 120km the new line follows the A1 Paris-Lille motorway very closely. This is not without problems for the constructors. Here, the line, on the left, has to dive under a service area near Peronne.**
Rail Info Collection

Left: **One of the last major SNCF lines to be electrified will be Paris-Caen-Cherbourg, which will be completed in 1995. During the summer of 1989 No BB 67551 is seen at Lisieux with the Saturday 12.08 Caen-Paris St Lazare service.** *Rail Info Collection*

Left: **Soon to be superseded by TGV-Nord rakes, a Dunkerque-Arras express, formed by four Corail coaches and hauled by No BB 16014, arrives at Bethune.** Rail Info Collection

Below left: **Another 'Cinderella' Intercity route with slow journey times and a doubtful future is Calais-Lille-Metz-Basel. Here 'Sybic' No 26039 prepares to leave Lille with the 07.26 train for Mulhouse in July 1991. The train averages only 80km/h between Lille and Metz.** Rail Info Collection

Prestige Services

Since 1957, when the Trans Europe Express brand name was created, SNCF has operated prestige international services usually at the highest average speeds and formed of the most comfortable rolling stock. TEE services were all First Class and represented the best of European rail travel for 30 years. However, in the face of erosion of the high quality end of the market by air, a new two-class network of services known as EuroCity superseded TEE in 1987. In order to qualify for the EuroCity title, trains have to be formed of air conditioned stock with dining facilities, and must meet strict quality criteria of comfort, speed and punctuality. The initial network of 26 pairs of trains had expanded to 75 by 1990. SNCF has participated fully in the development of the network and is certain to feature strongly in further expansion.

In recent years, SNCF has made great efforts to seduce the First Class traveller on internal services. Recent advertising promoting upgrading from Second was generally successful, with 5-20% increases in passenger numbers common — it must be said that at 50% above Second, SNCF First Class fares are still approximately half of BR full Second prices.

Design of accommodation recently took a great leap forward with the introduction of TGV-Atlantique in which plush seats are arranged either in classic face-to-face positions in open coaches or in semi-compartments which combine accessibility with intimacy. TGV-A units also have an eight-seat compartment fitted for video-screening, which is aimed at groups of business people desiring on-board meeting facilities.

In April 1991, a new First Class product, known as *Euraffaires*, was launched on the Paris-Strasbourg route. Coaches (transferred from former TEE Grand Confort vehicles) offer a very high standard of accommodation similar to that in TGV-A First Class with mixed semi-compartment and open accommodation. The 'Euraffaires' service also includes very high standard catering plus First Class only lounges in principal stations.

One of the most refreshing recent improvements to life as a rail passenger

Projected Intercity Traffic

	1988	1989	1990	1991	1992	1993	1994	1995
Total Intercity Traffic	47.8	48.8	49.9	51.4	52.0	54.1	58.4	62.1
Of which TGV	10.5	11.5	15.2	18.9	20.5	23.1	29.2	34.0

Figures in billion passenger km

but since 1945 progress has been continuous. As early as 1946, SNCF started to introduce standard passenger coaches throughout the network, replacing very varied designs with a modern metal-bodied design, known as DEV. From 1960, new designs known as US and UIC came into service but it was not until 1975 that a sea change of rolling stock design occurred with the introduction of Corail stock. Corail (COmfort-RAIL) coaches were the first passenger vehicles, apart from First Class-only designs, to feature air-conditioning, and brought new standards of ride and silence to the passenger environment.

The second element of post-war development has been speed. SNCF created a speed record of 331km/h in 1955, and two years later the first electric locomotives capable of regular 160km/h operation entered service. The BB 9200 (1,500V dc), BB 16000 (25kV ac) and BB 25200 (dual-voltage) generation of locomotives were to become the élite traction of the 1960s. After a period of experiments, regular 200km/h running was introduced on the Paris-Toulouse route in 1967 and later on Paris-Bordeaux. These routes, worked by the stunning Class CC 6500 electrics, remained the mainstay of 200km/h running for almost 20 years. In the late 1980s other schemes, involving elimination of level crossings and introduction of cab-signalling, allowed upgrading to 200km/h. These included the Rhône valley line between Valence and Avignon for TGV working and Le Mans-Nantes.

SNCF now systematically upgrades conventional lines to 200km/h (220km/h for TGVs) where economically justified, particularly on lines to be used by TGVs. Several schemes to raise speeds to these levels are included in SNCF's strategic high-speed plan and may well be suitable where a TGV line is not economically feasible.

Such increases in speed have been aided by the continual and regular electrification of the network since the war. Now that the Paris-Caen-Cherbourg line is being electrified, only one French main line, that from Paris Est to Belfort via Troyes, remains diesel worked. Unless regional bodies are prepared to finance the investment, this line is never likely to see electric traction, as the TGV-Rhine/Rhône project will drain a major part of through traffic from the line.

Left: **Night travel is an important market in France where distances of 700-1,000km are common. Here No CC 6501 is seen at Avignon with a southbound motorail train in June 1987.** *Rail Info Collection*

Below left: **One of the more recent innovations aimed at attracting families to travel by rail is the concept of 'Espace Enfants'. Here a group of youngsters enjoy the facilities provided in one of the 10 Corail coaches converted for the purpose.** *SNCF*

in France has been the virtual elimination of the ticket window queue. The busiest stations now have 'Dagober' touch screen terminals which issue tickets and reservations, accepting coins or credit cards in payment. But SNCF philosophy is that potential passengers must not be obliged to come to a station for information and tickets and that SNCF should go out to the customer wherever possible. Thus, SNCF is opening large numbers of ticket shops in High Streets and shopping centres and has taken full advantage of information technology in order to decentralise these services.

It is now possible to obtain much passenger service information using Minitel (see inset). Intending passengers can dial the Minitel number on their

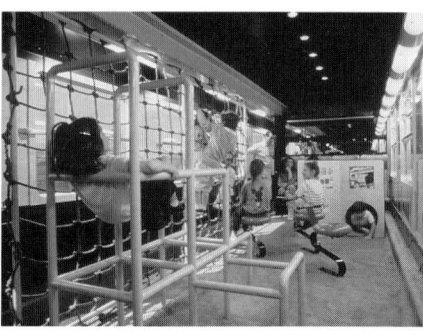

phone then connect the terminal when they hear a tone. They then type 'SNCF' to obtain a variety of services. For example, if the user wants to make a rail journey from St Etienne to Paris, he requests the timetable for this link on the day he wishes to travel. All direct trains or possibilities by changing will be shown and he can ask for greater detail of the one which suits him best. It is then possible to reserve a seat (if capacity remains) on the Lyon-Paris train (a TGV) specifying the type of accommodation required — First/Second, smoking or not. Once a final selection has been made, Minitel gives the user a reservation code number. The user then either pays for the tickets by post or collects them from the nearest station. SNCF is now experimenting with a credit card reader attached to the Minitel which will allow immediate payment 'at home',although initially this is for companies only.

SNCF has found that passengers are increasingly put off by breaking their journey in Paris. This has often been unavoidable in the past due to the nature of the SNCF network, which has relatively few transversal routes and even fewer through services. However, during the 1980s attempts were made to reduce the problem by the introduction of a small number of trains avoiding Paris although passing through its suburbs on freight lines. The Rouen/Lille-Lyon TGV services are a good example of this approach. The logical continuation of this policy is the construction of the Paris by-pass *Ligne à Grande Vitesse*. Future British users of the Channel Tunnel will particularly appreciate this line, which will allow journeys from London to the south of France, and other popular destinations without descending in Paris.

During the 1980s, SNCF targeted families as an under-developed market, particularly for long journeys. In order to provide play facilities for young children, 10 Corail coaches were converted into *Espace Enfants* vehicles, in which around one-third of the coach became a play area with a climbing frame and other amusements. Having tried out this facility with the aid of my three-year-old, I find it unfortunate that more coaches have not been converted. Although a space is provided on TGV-Atlantique trains where seats can be folded up to form a play space, nothing is offered in the way of a distraction to children. However, both TGV-A rakes and certain other trains now have baby changing and bottle-warming facilities. A financial incitement to family travel is provided by the 'Kiwi' card, which gives a 50% reduction to the holder and accompanying persons. This is actually established in the name of the child, and allows any adult, even those outside the family, to travel with him or her.

With distances of 700-1,200km between large towns common in France, night travel is an integral part of the rail offer. Although the speed of day travel is rising dramatically with the expansion of the TGV network, gaining a day by travelling at night will continue to be part of the French way of life. The evolution of couchette and sleeper coaches has followed that of day vehicles and has reached a very high standard of comfort, ride and silence with the current Corail stock.

Night travel is particularly common amongst young people who are studying or serving in the army a long way from home. With low budgets, many simply occupy a compartment in order to lie down full length. In order to provide this market with an alternative, SNCF introduced 20 *Cabine 8* vehicles, converted from Corail stock, in 1986. These offer eight semi-reclining seats per compartment and, unlike a couchette, are accessible without a surcharge. Although a moderate success, SNCF was concerned that, unlike couchette stock, where the berths can be folded away to make a six-seat day compartment, *Cabine 8* vehicles were restricted to night-time use. In order to tackle this problem, a number of Corail coaches were fitted with reclining seats in 1990 and put onto services such as Strasbourg-Ventimiglia and Metz-Nice.

Minitel

At a time when the train has pushed past the 500km/h (300mph) barrier, and in a book dealing with SNCF, it might be expected that this author would praise the TGV as the greatest French invention of the late 20th century. Unfortunately, TGV is pipped at the post by another bright idea which has changed the lives of French folk even more — the MINITEL. This small screen and keyboard is connected to the telephone system and comes free to all telephone subscribers. Services are paid for by the minute partly to France Telecom and partly to the provider of the service.

The response of customers has been so positive that almost all walks of French life now provide services, including weather forecasts, road congestion monitoring and, perhaps the most useful of all, a free of charge telephone directory which finds a telephone number and address in less than a second and which can list all subscribers of a given surname in a whole *département*. SNCF has not been slow to use this medium of communication. It is now possible for a potential traveller to receive timetable information between all major stations, then to reserve a seat, couchette or sleeping berth on a selected train. As the possibilities provided by a new reservations computer, SOCRATE, starting from 1992, become even greater, MINITEL will become an even more important tool for sales staff.

TGV

Projected New High Speed LInes included in the *Schéma Directeur*						
	Traffic Growth (million passengers pa)			Cost of Project (FF billion)		
Project	Before	After	Increase	Infrastructure	Rolling Stock	Rate of Return
Aquitaine	14.7	20.1	37%	2.2	0.9	7.6%
Auvergne	2.9	3.9	37%	4.6	1.3	3.1%
Bretagne	9.1	12.2	34%	5.7	0.8	7.4%
Est	7.4	14.5	96%	22.0	6.3	4.3%
Grand-Sud	3.7	5.3	42%	5.7	0.9	5.0%
Interconnection Sud	12.6	13.4	7%	3.3	0.2	8.2%
Trans-Alpine	8.4	14.7	75%	21.5*	5.5*	6.0%
Limousin	3.3	4.0	21%	5.3	1.4	2.4%
Provence-Côte d'Azur	15.9	23.4	47%	17.8	2.0	9%
Languedoc-Rousillon	5.8	9.5	65%	14.4	3.7	7.1%
Midi-Pyrénées	2.3	3.3	44%	8.4	—	5.5%
Normandie	5.5	7.1	29%	10.1	1.5	0.1%
Picardie	13.5	14.4	7%	6.3	—	4.8%
Rhine-Rhône	9.5	15.3	61%	17.8	4.3	5.9%

*Estimated French contribution
Total costs including Italian contribution (24.8+9.3) 33.1 billion francs
SOURCE: *La Vie Du Rail*

I make no apologies for the size of the section in this book devoted to the future TGV network and trains. Any book about SNCF at this time must take account of the complete domination of policy by TGV developments. Perhaps the story of the TGV (Train à Grande Vitesse — High Speed Train) is familiar to all modern rail professionals and enthusiasts by now; Brian Perren's *Modern Railways Special: TGV* and Murray Hughes' excellent book *RAIL 300* are good reference guides. However, perhaps a quick recap is necessary.

The construction of a new high-speed line (*Ligne à Grande Vitesse* or LGV) between Paris and Lyon came out of the impending saturation of the existing (indirect and very curvy) line via Dijon. The argument in favour of a completely new line, built for passenger trains only, was similar to that in favour of a motorway: one can go on building by-passes to traffic black spots for years but a completely new road will be cheaper and give a better quality result in the long term.

Although theoretically an economically sound project, the construction of the first LGV was an act of faith, and perhaps typical of French vision. That further LGV projects have followed quickly is due to the overwhelming success of the first line and the new-found enthusiasm of the French for high-speed rail. At the inauguration of the LGV Sud-Est, President Mitterand announced plans for the Atlantique line, whose two branches opened in 1989 and 1990, and since then proposals have come thick and fast.

Before the opening of the Sud-Est LGV, unit No 26 clocked up 380km/h in 1981, but this was later surpassed by the German ICE prototype with 406.9km/h in 1988. It was clear that the French would not let the matter rest there, but even seasoned rail commentators must have been surprised when a TGV-A unit No 325 was pushed up to 482.4km/h in late 1989, then to an incredible 515.3km/h (well over 300mph) in May 1990. The importance of this record must not be underestimated. Pushing the frontiers of steel wheel on steel rail traction this far not only shows that higher day-to-day speeds are possible with future TGVs, but also it cocks a snook at current efforts of high speed magnetic levitation enthusiasts. The TGV is the perfect marriage of the use of existing rail infrastructure to penetrate to the heart of cities, with high-speed running on completely new lines when economically justified.

As a result of experience with ultra high speed running, SNCF will be able to aim for a 320km/h maximum for TGV-Nord. In the longer term, they are talking about averaging 1,000km in three hours, a feat which will mean a maximum of at least 350km/h. Having experienced the billiard table smooth ride of the LGV Atlantique, I am sure this is technically possible.

The French are now convinced of the merits of a high speed rail link and now every major town in France wants its own TGV. Furthermore, the development of high-speed in West Germany (with

Left: **Soon after the start of test running in the summer of 1989 TGV-Atlantique rake No 310 leaves Paris Montparnasse.**
Rail Info Collection

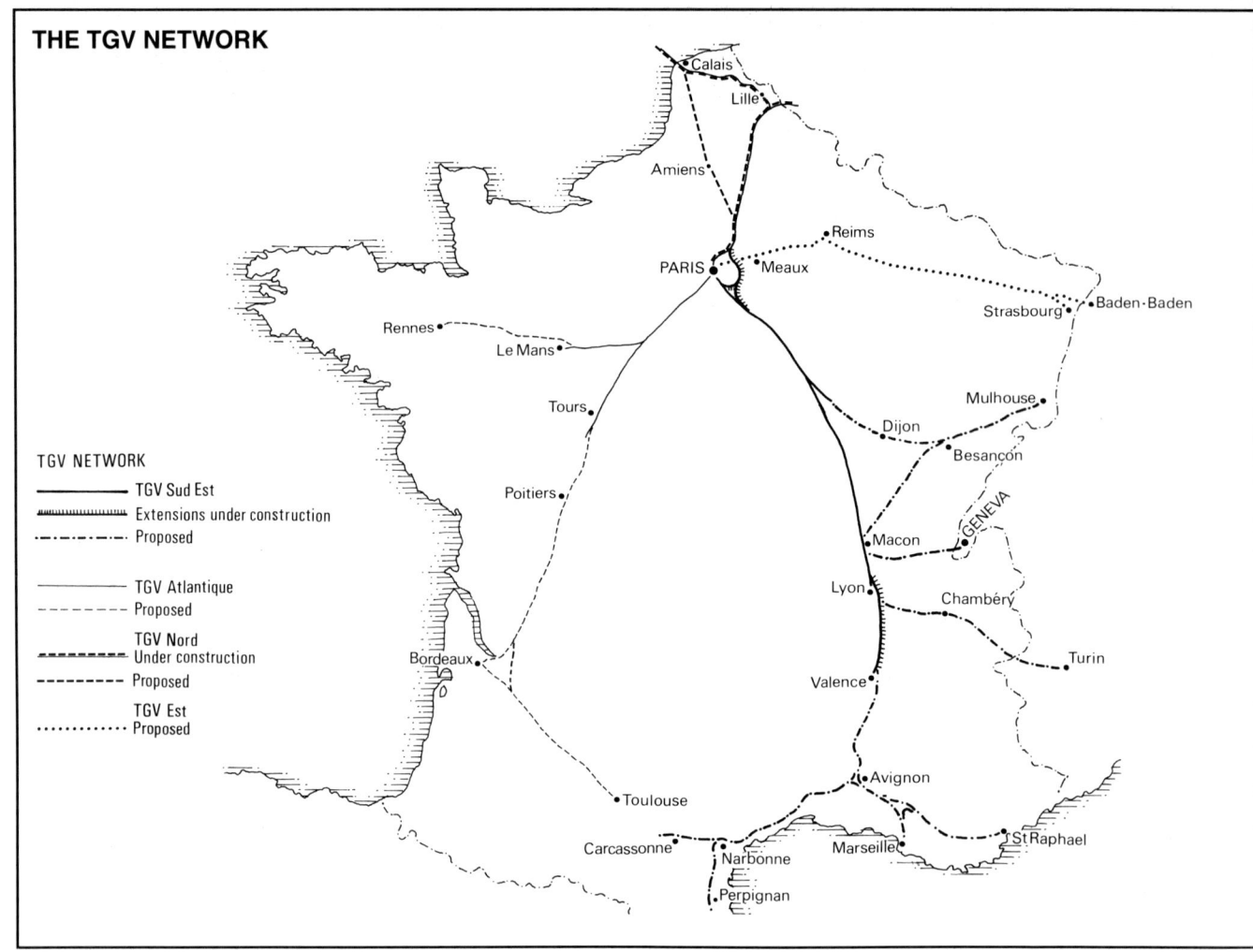

THE TGV NETWORK

TGV NETWORK
- TGV Sud Est
- Extensions under construction
- Proposed
- TGV Atlantique
- Proposed
- TGV Nord
- Under construction
- Proposed
- TGV Est
- Proposed

ICE), Italy (with the Pendolino and ETR500), Spain (with a version of the French TGV), even the UK, where a high-speed Channel Tunnel link has yet to take shape, led to proposals for a European high-speed network at the end of the 1980s. SNCF was quick to stress that by the end of the century, its own TGV network would be central to a wider European system.

At the beginning of 1990, SNCF submitted a report called *Schéma Directeur des Lignes à Grande Vitesse* — strategic plan for high-speed lines. Although this is more a statement of intent than a concrete proposal, it does point the way towards the SNCF of the 21st century. Several of the projects should be mentioned strictly in the conditional tense as it is doubtful they will ever be built.

After the débâcle surrounding the attempts to promote the Channel Tunnel high-speed link in Kent, many British readers will be wondering why it has seemed so easy to push the TGV projects through in France. The most important factor is certainly the government backing for SNCF implicit in the *Société Nationale's* contract with the state. But the simple fact is that it has not been as easy as is sometimes stated and the task seems to be getting increasingly difficult.

In a country the size of France, it was quite easy to secure routes for the LGV Sud-Est and Atlantique — not a single town of any size can be spotted along their length. In most cases, SNCF was negotiating with moderately down-at-heel farmers who gladly exchanged a sliver of land for a new tractor. In addition, since the construction of the first LGV, SNCF has increased the budget for environmental protection measures and on the LGV-Nord, this should reach 15% of the total. On the LGV-Atlantique, there was the well publicised creation of a new pond for frogs whose habitat lay in the new line's path!

The latest LGV projects are providing SNCF with many more headaches, particularly as they pass through more populated areas. Residents in the suburbs of Lille have forced the LGV-Nord underground in several places, upping the budget considerably and delaying the line's opening. Protesters against the TGV-Méditerranée route regularly blocked lines for several months during 1990 and have forced a change of route which will reduce the project's rate of return from 12% to 9%. Despite these efforts by SNCF, they continued protests throughout 1991 although now without the support of local mayors. However, most efforts have been to persuade the TGV to pass through a region or town rather than by-pass it. Amiens fought a losing battle with Lille over the TGV-Nord route, whilst several regions and towns, such as La Rochelle, have put up the funds for electrification which will allow direct TGV services. Most recently, normally sane citizens of certain Brittany towns have lain across the tracks in attempts to have the TGV stop at their station!

FUTURE TGV-SUD-EST EXTENSION

TGV-Méditerranée (Provence-Côte d'Azur)

When the initial timetable was introduced on the TGV-Sud-Est line, Marseille and Montpellier were the furthest south the new trains reached, taking under five hours. Good onward connections were provided from Marseille to the Côte d'Azur (French Riviera) resorts. At the time, SNCF considered that TGVs were not suitable for longer journeys and that the expensive trains would be wasted on the snaky Riviera route which does not allow high speeds. However, the decision was met with criticism, and SNCF introduced first a service to Toulon, then later to Nice — a seven hour journey from Paris.

Left: **Emphasising the superb new engineering characteristic of the TGV projects, a TGV-Sud-Est rake is seen passing Flagy on 24 July 1986.**
Paul D. Shannon

Below left: **A total of 109 TGV units were acquired for the Sud Est project and a further 97 for the TGV-Atlantique. With two power cars and eight trailers, each of the TGV-Sud Est sets, such as No 15 illustrated here, can accommodate 386 passengers. The TGV-Atlantique sets, with 10 trailer cars, have seating for a total of 485.** *SNCF*

Traffic on the Côte d'Azur route has been extremely buoyant and an extension of the Sud-Est LGV became an early priority. SNCF is therefore constructing a 115km extension which leaves the present LGV north of Lyon, by-passing the city and rejoining the existing line just north of Valence. The first section of the line, which will serve Lyon Satolas airport and connect into the Lyon-Grenoble line, will be opened in 1992, allowing reductions of 20 minutes Paris-Grenoble and 18 minutes Paris-Chambéry, just in time for the Winter Olympics at Albertville in the French Alps. The section onwards to Valence will be completed in 1994, allowing cuts of around half an hour in Paris-Marseille/Montpellier times.

At the beginning of 1990, SNCF announced the route of the 340km TGV-Méditerranée, which will extend the LGV as far as Marseille and Fréjus on the line to Nice. However, the route provoked virulent protests from the local population, particularly second home owners in the area of Mont Sainte-Victoire which was immortalised on canvas by Cézanne. Opposition reached a crescendo in summer 1990 when protesters blocked stations in the region for many weeks running. SNCF responded by appointing a 'Mr TGV-Méditerranée' — Max Querrien — in the hope of smoothing the project's passage. After long consultation with all concerned parties, a revised route was accepted by the Transport Minister at the beginning of 1991. In principle, this is the final stage before SNCF starts studies resulting in a 'declaration of public utility' which sets the final seal on the project. The line is planned for completion in 1997.

The new line will continue south from the end of the Lyon by-pass extension at St-Marcel-lès-Valence running to the east of the existing line. It will then head southwest, passing almost through the bounds of Pierrelatte nuclear power station before crossing the 'classic' line near Lapalud. Here a chord will allow trains to enter Avignon from the north via Orange. The line will then cross the Rhône twice, carefully avoiding the Châteauneuf-du-Pape vineyards. Just to the west of the Avignon urban area, the line will divide into the Montpellier and Marseille branches, with a southern chord forming a triangle.

The Marseille branch will then skirt Avignon by the south, where a new station is proposed, with a chord giving direct access to the papal city's existing station. After passing close to Cavaillon, the Marseille and Fréjus branches will separate near Saint-Cannat, close to which a new station will be built to serve Aix-en-Provence. The eastern branch will join up with the existing Côte d'Azur line just to the west of St Raphaël, although SNCF is examining the possibility of extending it further towards Cannes.

The new line will bring Marseille to within a flat three hours of Paris and Nice to within three hours 40 minutes. SNCF predicts that traffic will more than double from 9.5 million in 1988 to 23.4 million passenger journeys in 1997. Indeed, of all the TGV projects in the pipeline, TGV-Méditerranée presents by far the best rate of return. However, initial predictions of a 12% return are now reduced to 9%, given an investment of FF 25 billion including rolling stock against the FF 20 billion originally envisaged.

TGV-Méditerranée (Languedoc-Roussillon)

A logical extension of the TGV-Méditerrané is towards Languedoc-Roussillon, the tourist and wine-growing region which has Montpellier as its capital. SNCF announced plans in November 1990 for a line which would leave the Valence-Marseille LGV close to Avignon, passing close to Nîmes and Montpellier before turning south to Perpignan and ultimately across the Spanish frontier. Montpellier would thus be three hours and Perpignan three hours 40 minutes from Paris. If Spanish Railways, (RENFE) plan for a standard gauge high-speed line is implemented, this will give a Paris-Barcelona timing of four hours 30 minutes. The line would be opened in 1997 or 1998.

The 295km line would cost FF 14.8 billion to build, and with a projected increase in passengers of almost 4 million a year, this gives a rate of return of only 5.9%, which itself depends on the Barcelona extension. This does not satisfy SNCF investment criteria but it is highly likely that the Languedoc-Roussillon Region will contribute the missing funds.

TGV-Grand-Sud

The Languedoc-Rousillon LGV also forms part of the Grand-Sud project. Given the extension of the LGV-

Right: **With the telephoto lens emphasising the gradients, a TGV-Sud-Est rake is seen passing the junction at Pasily, where the branch to Dijon leaves the main Paris-Lyon route, on 23 July 1986.** *Paul D. Shannon*

Below right: **A close-up of the articulation unit between two of the TGV-Sud-Est trailer cars.** *SNCF*

Atlantique from Bordeaux to Toulouse (see below) relatively little additional construction would be necessary to provide a much improved Bordeaux-Marseille/Côte d'Azur link. The missing pieces would be provided by upgrading Toulouse-Bram for 220km/h running, then constructing 105km of new line from Bram to Narbonne. The resulting journey time reductions are significant but the project would again require finance from the Regions concerned as its rate of return would be only 3.4%.

TGV-Rhine-Rhône
This project totalling 425km, which is predicted to have around a 6% rate of return would give a branch off the Paris-Lyon LGV near Montbard, serving Dijon, passing close to Dôle, Besançon and Belfort, then linking into the 'classic' network near Mulhouse. This would allow accelerations between Paris and Basel/Zürich as well as the aforementioned towns. A southern link off this line would join the Sud-Est LGV near Macon and allow TGVs to link Strasbourg and northern Switzerland with the south of France. So far many possible routing variants exist particularly for the southern link. For clarity, only one has been indicated on the map.

TGV-Trans-Alpine
The most spectacular of the present projects is that which would link the Sud-Est LGV to the Italian sistema ad alta velocita high-speed system. The line would leave the Sud-Est LGV at Satolas (Lyon airport) passing close to Chambéry where there would be a station. Spectacular, because it will have to traverse the Alpine chain via a 54km long tunnel! This tunnel, between the Maurienne valley and Susa in Italy, would be the longest in the world, beating the Sikan tunnel in Japan by 2km. It is not surprising that the cost of the 201km (not including the 51km in Italy) line is almost as high as the 430km of the TGV-Est. Surprisingly, the estimated rate of return is as high as 5.6%. This is because passenger traffic would double and freight would benefit immensely by using the new tunnel — Modane-Turin is the busiest international route for freight in France with 8 million tonnes handled each year. It is probable that the project would go forward in two stages. First the Satolas-Chambéry line, which would in itself allow Paris-Turin times to be cut by

two hours. If and when the Alpine tunnel were completed, Paris-Turin would be reduced to three hours 5 minutes (six hours 21 minutes at present), with Milan possible in four hours 15 minutes and Venice in six hours.

Macon-Genève
Although not included in the strategic plan, Swiss Railways (SBB-CFF-FFS) are working with SNCF on the possibility of an LGV from Macon to Genève. This would allow a Paris-Genève time of little over 2hours, a great improvement on present trains (3 1/2 hr) which are handicapped by the tortuous route east of Bourg-en-Bresse. A study being carried out on behalf of the Swiss has costed the link at FF 13.25 billion (the region is very mountainous and will necessitate 34.5km of tunnel and restrict maximum speed to 230km/h) including the purchase of 20 tri-voltage TGVs. Given this only gives a rate of return of 4.8%, work could be staggered over a long period.

TGV-Nord
Perhaps the most interesting project to the British as the line will soon carry millions of us each year, the TGV-Nord was originally programmed ahead of the Atlantique project but was shelved as its economic success depended on the construction of the Channel Tunnel. This T-shaped line from Paris Nord to Lille with branches to the Channel Tunnel (thence London) and the Belgian frontier, and ultimately Brussels, is on schedule for completion at the same time as the Chunnel in June 1993 although there has been a small hiccup in the Lille area. TGV-Nord will be unique in being operated not only by the Three Capitals trains, TGV-R trains some capable of operation at 3,000V dc in Belgium and a third design for services to Amsterdam and Köln, but also double-deck TGVs, which will be necessary for domestic Paris-Lille traffic (see below).

The city of Amiens, by-passed by the TGV-Nord, much to the anger of Picardie, has been promised its own line but with no time scale fixed. When and if the Paris-Lille line approached saturation, a 165km cut-off line, known as TGV-Picard would be built via Amiens, shearing 17 minutes off Paris-

London times. However, one has to doubt whether this project has not been included more to calm Picard sensibilities than for any real commercial reason.

The Paris Interconnexion
Because it is a relatively short (102km) section of line, it is possible to neglect the Paris by-pass Interconnexion line, which is at present under construction to the east of the capital. However, this line represents a return on capital of 14% for SNCF and a revolution given the travel possibilities it will open up. Whereas Paris represents an almost obligatory break of journey at a European level at present, after opening in 1994, the Interconnexion will allow the Ile-de-France region to become the hub of a future European high-speed network. Thus in 1994, Brussels-Lyon will take a mere 3hr 40min direct against a present best of around six hours with an enforced descent, bags and all, into the Paris Métro after the first half of the journey.

The Paris by-pass will leave the LGV-Nord near Roissy-Charles de Gaulle airport, which will be served by a new central station (with connections to RER Line B), which will open up vast rail-air travel opportunities. The *Interconnexion* then runs roughly south, serving the future EuroDisneyland (interchange with RER Line A) before joining the LGV Sud-Est east of Melun new town. A triangle at Coubert and a chord to Valenton will allow trains from the north and south to link into the LGV-Atlantique at Massy, albeit with a short period of running at less than 100km/h on the *Grande Ceinture* freight line. The new chord will also allow a slight reduction in times for Sud-Est TGVs.

Interconnexion Sud
SNCF acknowledges that using the Grande Ceinture in order to link into the LGV-Atlantique is not ideal and has thus proposed a further Interconnexion line in the Schéma Directeur. The

Above: **The Class CC 72000 diesel-electrics are the most powerful diesel locomotives in service with SNCF. No 72008 passes La Bachellerie with the 14.19 Clermont Ferrand-Bordeaux service on 3 August 1989.** *Mike Hemming*

Below: **Shortly before arriving at Paris Gare de Lyon, a pair of TGV-Sud-Est rakes is seen passing through Villeneuve St Georges in July 1990. One unit originated in Avignon, the other in St Etienne.** *Rail Info Collection*

Top: **The interior of a First Class open trailer on the TGV-Atlantique.** *SNCF*

Above: **The interior of a Second Class trailer on the TGV-Atlantique. As with the First Class trailer, the second generation of TGV units have improved seating compared with TGV-Sud-Est.** *SNCF*

Interconnexion Sud would be a 43km line leaving the LGV-A at Vaugrigneuse and joining the LGV Sud-Est near its present origin, Lieusaint. A 6km chord would form a triangle of the junction between the north Interconnexion and the LGV Sud-Est. The result would be savings of 21 minutes for Lyon-Nantes trains and 13 minutes on Lille-Bordeaux, for example. A new station would be built to serve the burgeoning new town of Melun-Sénart. This Interconnexion does satisfy SNCF criteria, with a rate of return exceeding 8%, but no time scale has been fixed for its construction.

TGV-EST

With TGV Sud-Est in service for almost 10 years and being extended southwards, TGV-A recently opened and TGV-Nord plus the Paris Interconnexion under construction, present interest centres on TGV-Est. Logically this is the next spoke of the wheel centred on Paris. Strasbourg and the equally weighted cities of Nancy and Metz in the Lorraine region are the principal destinations, with an eastward connection possible into Germany and newly liberated Eastern Europe. However, things are not so simple. Although the project is backed to the hilt by the eastern French regions, the economic argument for the line is not proven. A return on capital of only 4.3% is predicted, far from satisfactory for SNCF. Philippe Essig, a former President of SNCF, is charged with organising financing, and had come up with a formula involving Central Government, the Regions, SNCF and probably the EC. In late 1990, the French government baulked at paying the FF 6.6 billion request and asked Essig to review his plans. Any further problems could make the TGV Rhine-Rhône project look more attractive – Strasbourg and Alsace being reached from Paris Gare de Lyon via Dijon, leaving the Lorraine region high and dry!

Despite uncertainty over finance, the route of TGV-Est is already more or less fixed. Leaving the present Paris Est-Strasbourg route at Vaires, the new line would be largely to the north of the present one. New stations would be built near Reims and between Nancy and Metz. The line would join the existing alignment close to Strasbourg. Projected journey times from Paris would be Reims 45 minutes, Metz-Nancy 1hr 30min, and Strasbourg 1hr 50min. Four hours are necessary for the latter journey at present. Various chords off the LGV are possible and are subject to study. One possibility would be a link allowing Luxembourg-Metz-Strasbourg-Basel TGV service. The Strasbourg-Basel line has been the theatre of many high-speed runs in the past, and would allow 220km/h with little modernisation.

EXTENSIONS TO TGV-ATLANTIQUE

TGV-Bretagne

The northern branch of the TGV-A line to Le Mans opened in September 1989, and the southern section to Tours exactly a year later. Traffic projections are already being exceeded, and SNCF is not satisfied to rest on its laurels as far as its Atlantic coast services are concerned. Included in the *Schéma Directeur* is an extension of the northern branch to Rennes, thus avoiding Le Mans. This would reduce Paris-Rennes from 2hr to 1hr 26min, and allow Brest and Quimper to be attained in around 3hr 15min. On the other hand, SNCF had no plans originally to extend the LGV to Nantes. This is because Le Mans-Nantes has already been upgraded for 220km/h, and due to the lack of important destinations beyond Nantes. However, the Schéma Directeur has been revised to include such a line, which would cut 13 min off present best times and give a 5.4% rate of return.

TGV-Aquitaine

SNCF does not see Tours as the logical end of the southern branch of the LGV Atlantique either. Despite the expensive upgrading of Tours-Bordeaux for up to 220km/h, the construction of a completely new 361km line to Bordeaux and onward to Dax would give a 7.6% rate of return — handsome compared with TGV-Est, for example. Bordeaux-Paris times would fall to 2hr 6min, with the Spanish frontier at around 3hr 15min from the French capital. Before TGV-A, this run took around seven hours!

Left: **On a sunny day in October 1990 TGV-Atlantique unit No 349 arrives at Paris Montparnasse station with the first Nantes service of the day.** *Rail Info Collection*

Below left: **No BB 15052** *Cambrai* **waits to depart from Nancy with a train of Corail stock for Strasbourg. Class BB 15000 is one of Alsthom's very successful designs of electric locomotive and was followed by Classes BB 7200 (1,500V dc) and BB 22200 (dual voltage). The Paris Est-Strasbourg route is difficult to upgrade and thus the construction of TGV-Est is important for the future of the corridor.** *Rail Info Collection*

TGV-Midi-Pyrénées
From the beginning of the TGV-A Tours branch timetable, one train a day was provided between Paris and Toulouse via Bordeaux with a second added in September 1991. Despite the longer distance, a time of 5hr 7min was possible, almost an hour shorter than via the Limoges 'classic' route. With the extension of LGV-A to Bordeaux, this would come down to 3hr 40min. SNCF plans to go one better by building a branch off the LGV-A from Libourne to Toulouse, putting Toulouse at 2hr 48min from Paris; a veritable revolution for Toulouse, which has seen itself lose out in the rail speed stakes in recent years.

Other lines
Included in the Schéma Directeur are several other sections of high speed line with very low rates of return which one suspects are only included in the report to satisfy political aspirations — almost everyone in France now wants his own TGV! Lines included in this section should thus be spoken about strictly in the conditional tense.

TGV-Normandie
A line from Achères in the Paris suburbs to Rouen with a branch to Bernay on the line to Caen and Cherbourg, which will be electrified by 1994. This would reduce Paris-Rouen from 1hr 10min to 40 minutes and lop 20 minutes off Paris-Caen timings. The project has an estimated rate of return of 0.1% and so is not likely to be on anyone's shopping list.

TGV-Auvergne
Improving links to the hilly and sparsely-populated centre of France is somewhat problematical. Paris-Clermont Ferrand was recently electrified, but most trains still take over 3hr 30min for the 420km. A proposal by the Auvergne Region to build a link from Vichy to Montchanin on the LGV Sud-Est has not been accepted by SNCF due to lack of capacity, and because it misses out all intermediate stations. The Schéma Directeur includes a proposal for an LGV from Brétigny (on the Paris Austerlitz main line) to Gien, from whence the 'classic' line to Clermont would be upgraded for 220km/h running. Again an estimated rate of return of 3.1% rather condemns the project from the start.

TGV-Limousin
With the extension of the LGV Atlantique to Bordeaux and onwards to Toulouse, Limoges, the only city of great importance on the Toulouse 'classic' route, will be left in the wilderness. Thus, politicans in the Limousin Region are pressing for an LGV too. SNCF has proposed a mix of line improvements and new sections of LGV from Vierzon southwards. This project would give a return on capital of 2.4%. The poor potential of the present TGV-Auvergne and Limousin projects will certainly lead to further proposals in future, possibly leading to a common section of LGV between the two present lines. We shall have to watch and wait.

THE TGV UNITS
It was commonly stated on their introduction that TGVs were quite conventional articulated mulitiple-unit trains. Perhaps, but they were extremely sophisticated conventional trains, taking then state-of-the-art steel wheel on steel rail to its limits. A TGV-Sud-Est is basically two power cars, enclosing eight articulated trailers, whose outer bogies are also powered. The main fleet of 101 trains are dual-voltage, allowing use throughout the SNCF electrified network which is approximately half 1,500V dc and half 25kV ac 50Hz. Nine other units also operate off 15kV ac 16 2/3 Hz for use in Switzerland.

The interiors of TGV-Sud-Est rakes now seem a little down-beat and functional compared to the newly introduced TGV-A sets. Second Class seats are covered in dark green or blue plastic material, which is finally finding disfavour with SNCF, and will be replaced with more pleasant moquette in future.

After a good five years, experience with the Sud-Est rakes, and tests on prototype rake No 88, it was possible to make considerable improvements to TGV-A units. Use of synchronous three-phase motors allowed the number of powered axles to be reduced from 12 to eight at the same time as increasing the number of trailer cars from eight to 10. The same bogies with pneumatic suspension as were retro-fitted to Sud-Est sets give a near perfect ride at the increased maximum of 300km/h. TGV-A trains are also fitted with an on-board computer which controls and monitors all functions, being able to give fault-finding

19

Left: **With the electrification of Lyon-Strasbourg due for completion in 1995 this scene at Mouchard will be transformed. RTG 'Turbotrain' prepares to leave with the 15.36 Strasbourg-Lille, whilst an X2800 railcar arrives with a stopping train from Lyon to Besancon.** *Rail Info Collection*

Right: **More regular duty for a Chalindrey depot Class BB 25150. One of the Class, No 25162, is seen hauling a freight service near Lens in 1989. Leading the rake of freight wagons is one branded with the new SNCF 'FRET' logo. Note the new 'hollow' SNCF logo in contrast to BB 25185 illustrated above.** *Rail Info Collection*

Below right: **Introduced in 1967 and built until 1977, the 45 locomotives of Class BB 25150 were a development of the earlier Class BB 25100. Although a predominantly freight class, a number are used on passenger services to the Alps. No BB 25185 is seen in February 1985 heading the 10.13 St Gervais-Lyon service, with the snow covered peaks in the background.** *Rail Info Collection*

diagnostics to the driver via a cab screen and keyboard.

For the passenger, particularly in First Class, the real revolution is in a greatly rethought interior. Tasteful moquettes are used in both classic open and new 'Club' semi-compartment accommodation, whilst an eight-seat compartment with video facilities is available for on-board meetings or entertaining. In Second, priority is given to the family, with a play area plus face-to-face seating around nursery facilities.

During late 1991 the first of 80 TGV-R units will be delivered. R stands for *Réseau* (network), indicating that they are conceived to work more or less throughout the network. They will be similar to TGV-A trains, but reduced to eight trailers to allow them to match Sud-Est platform lengths. Interior comfort will be improved, with reclining seats, to take account of the preponderance of longer journeys such as Nantes-Lyon or Lille-Marseille. A second tranche of 30 three-voltage units will be delivered later. These will operate off Belgian 3,000V dc as well as the standard SNCF 1,500V dc and 25kV 50Hz ac systems, thus allowing through trains from Brussels to the south of France.

Leaving aside TGV-R and the multi-voltage 'Three Capitals' trains needed for Channel Tunnel services, the main innovation will be *double-deck* TGVs which will almost certainly be capable of 320 if not 350km/h! Double-deck capacity is considered necessary on the Paris-Lille route, already with a roughly hourly service of 12-16 coach trains, where traffic is expected to double. The 'Three Capitals' 30 exceptional trains have now been ordered for Channel Tunnel services between the three capitals of London, Paris and Brussels, and warrant several pages to themselves. Although not exactly TGVs, they will be largely derived from the French units for the simple reason that nobody else in Europe has a proven fleet of high-speed electric trains. However, the trains will have many unique features. They will operate off French 25kV ac and Belgian 3,000V dc overhead plus British Southern Region 750V dc third rail. Each unit will have two power cars and 18 trailers, divided into two articulated rakes with cabs at their inner ends, so that they can be driven separately in the event of an incident. Asynchronous three-phase traction motors will produce 14,000kW under 25kV for speeds of up to 300km/h.

During 1990, SNCF announced a FF 500 million programme of research into the further development of the TGV. Included in the terms of reference was consideration of a tilting version of the record breaking train. However, despite tilting trains finding favour in many parts of Europe, SNCF appears to pooh-pooh the idea of a tilting TGV. Whether this is for political reasons — not wishing to jeopardise the campaign for funds to build new high speed lines — remains to be seen.

THE EFFECT OF TGV ON THE REMAINING SYSTEM

Although the development of TGV services has been an undoubted success both technically and financially for SNCF, the effect on the overall network has quite often been negative. In most cases, replacement of 'classic' trains by TGVs has been accompanied by rationalisation of stopping patterns to optimise TGV speeds between major stations. Thus, the introduction of TGVs on the Paris-Brest service has brought drastic time reductions to Rennes, St Brieuc and Le Mans, but also severe cuts in direct services to Versailles, Chartres, Laval, Vitré, Guingamp and Morlaix.

A future example of the negative TGV effect is that of Douai. At present, Douai (a conurbation of 200,000 inhabitants) is served by 12 direct trains per day to Paris (in around two hours), as all Lille-Paris trains call. In order to exploit the LGV Nord to the full, Lille will have a non-stop TGV service to Paris from 1993, leaving Douai with six trains a day (starting back from Valenciennes) albeit with a one hour journey time. Although this is already a handicap on the direct journey concerned, it also means reduced connectional possibilities which may condemn rail for a particular journey.

Tours finds itself in a similar situation. At present served in part by direct TGVs and partly by connections off Paris-Bordeaux trains, the Loire Valley capital stands to lose out when long-distance TGVs are diverted via the future TGV-Aquitaine line which avoids the Tours area. Not only will the choice of trains to/from Paris be reduced, but also the number of trains going south towards Bordeaux. Finally, Tours' city fathers fear that in future longer distance trains will be allocated the prime Paris arrival/departure slots, with the Tours terminating service fitting in where possible.

NON-TGV PASSENGER SERVICE PROSPECTS

With such great concentration on building new high-speed lines, what of the future of 'classic' express passenger trains in France, particularly those on transversal lines not serving Paris? As

an observer of and user of SNCF services for the last eight years, I find this a preoccupying question.

Many railwaymen, their unions and consumer groups plus even the regional councils have been talking of a two-speed network for some time and of a management obsession with its symbol of virility, the TGV, traffic on 'classic' express services has been stagnant for the last few years, overall growth depending entirely on TGV.

SNCF managers of course deny this accusation — they argue that with FF 43.5 billion to be invested in TGV lines and stock over the period 1990-94 compared with FF 37.6 billion for the 'classic' network, the two are being treated equally. The fact that TGV will represent half of all Intercity traffic by the end of this period seems to justify the figure. However, TGV traffic will be well below half of all rail traffic once regional passenger, Paris suburban, freight and parcels are included.

Close examination of 'classic' investment also reveals that investment in electrification and level crossing elimination is mainly to allow TGVs to use the lines — Poitiers-La Rochelle and Rennes-Quimper, for example. The majority of station refurbishments follow this pattern. Clearly the conclusion is that it pays to live on a line served by TGV.

From my conversations with SNCF managers, I detect a lack of interest in services which are not or will not in future be operated by TGV. Medium distance services which do not serve Paris are rarely considered as having potential and are not actively promoted. For me these are the 'forgotten' SNCF passenger services, which are neither crack expresses nor TER (regional expresses).

An example of a total lack of an overall management plan is the Amiens-Rouen line. On electrification in September 1984 the Lille-Amiens-Rouen service (two trains each way per day) was considerably accelerated and upgraded using Corail stock, timings allowing good connections at Rouen to and from Le Havre. After initial publicity, the service has been completely ignored. Nothing has been done to advertise the potential for tourism in Amiens or Rouen. What's more, no Lille-Le Havre pocket timetables are available and the official SNCF timetable does not show several Lille-Rouen possibilities involving changes at Amiens. Stopping services have also been poorly organised. Despite costly electrification (FF 457 million in 1984 — note that the line only carries six passenger trains per day in each direction!), the majority of services were still formed of 1960s vintage Class X4500 DMU (maximum speed 120km/h with very sluggish acceleration) until 1990 when they were replaced by Class X6300 EMUs. Although these units cut 2 to 6 minutes off the 121km journey through their superior acceleration, they cannot be considered ideal for the task. Built in the late 1960s for Paris suburban services, with high-density bench seating, they are also restricted to 120km/h. Unlike Class 307s on the Leeds-Doncaster service, they are not considered a stop-gap measure, as nothing is programmed to replace them.

The transfer of responsibilities for local trains to the Regions has in some ways made the situation worse. Medium distance services which according to SNCF have little potential are taken over by the Regions. In some cases the service is then broken up, with trains terminating at the regional boundary instead of continuing a little further to a large town which would seem the natural terminus. Thus in certain cases 'Balkanisation' is taking place.

The 'all TGV' mentality can be seen in a lack of action on other fronts. The 1990-1994 SNCF Plan has a lot to say about TGV development, but precious little about other services, which will still account for around half of all traffic at the end of the plan. The Plan states that line speeds and service frequencies will be raised where demand merits, but also that a small number of very lightly used lines will be closed. Leaving aside TGV, the only lines of action included are on promoting international services, especially in the EuroCity network, and the improvement of information, ticketing and reservation services to the client. Other pressing matters such as refurbishment of Corail stock, now a 15-year-old design, and new sleeper and couchette stock are not mentioned.

Regional Passenger Services

Local services (often called Omnibus — meaning stopping at every village halt) have long been the Cinderella of the SNCF network, functioning with hand-me-down rolling stock, hauled by locomotives filling in between more glamorous work. Disaffection with them, both from customers and management, was clearly evident in declining patronage and never-changing timetables. Saving these services — one could never call them a network — from sure demise has been a long haul which started around the beginning of the 1970s. The creation of 22 regional councils was certainly one of the main spurs. Pilot schemes and partial agreements, concentrating on improving services on certain corridors — in Lorraine with 'Metrolor' Thionville-Metz-Nancy, in Provence-Alpes-Côte d'Azur with 'Metrazur' Cannes-Nice-Ventimiglia and in Rhône-Alpes with 'Stélyrail' Lyon-St Etienne, for example.

The embryonic nature of power and means of finance in the new Regions prevented important steps for some time but in the course of the 1970s certain limited agreements were made between the Regions and SNCF. The most important of these was in the Nord-Pas-de-Calais where the Region financed market studies, and then decided to invest FF 30 million (1978 prices) in 65 three-car push-pull rakes which were to replace all the ancient passenger stock being used on local services, between 1978 and 1981. In the 10 following years, train mileage has increased by 40%, whilst usage has jumped by 44%.

The most important spur to the reconsideration of the role of local services came in 1982 with a new law on decentralisation of powers concerning transport to the regions — *Loi d'orientation les transports intérieurs* (LOTI). This law defines three types of passenger service to be provided by SNCF:

- national services, which are decided upon by SNCF itself, taking into account government policy. In principle this network receives no financial support.
- regional services, over routes defined in Regional transport plans and organised by Regional councils.
- other regional services, which remain the responsibility of central government.

LOTI and the 1985 SNCF plan hailed a new era of partnership between SNCF and the Regions (see map). Three joint agreements were signed in 1984, and four in 1985, with 19 of the 22 Regions signed up by the end of 1989. The only exceptions are Ile-de-France (the Paris region) and Corsica which both have special status. Most agreements are for five years and cover all SNCF local services within the Region, which are then included in the Regional transport plan, which also includes bus routes. In a similar way to British Rail's relationship with the British Passenger Transport Authorities, SNCF becomes simply a supplier of rail services while the Region takes over the often difficult decisions on adapting services to demand, taking into account their policies.

In general, Regions signed up quickly because agreements brought no financial penalty in the short term. Another considerable encouragement was that, in the absence of agreement, it was probable that SNCF would have

Above left: **Although fast (capable of speeds of up to 160km/h) the Class Z 7300 (Z2) two-car EMUs have proved expensive for regional services. A pair of these units, headed by No Z 17353, are seen at Tours.**
Rail Info Collection

Left: **Regional push-pull 'RRR' stock in the yellow livery of the 'Lorraine' Region is seen at Nancy with a 'Metrolor' train from Thionville on 25 April 1991.**
Rail Info Collection

taken the axe to local services, leaving little left to sign for. On signature, and for five years, the existing service pattern and its financial situation became the reference service, with the deficit paid into SNCF coffers by central government. If receipts then vary, the Region must compensate SNCF for any fall, or will receive any surplus for re-investment. Improvements to service frequencies, rarely covered by new receipts, must be compensated by reductions elsewhere, or by a permanent contribution from the Region. This usually means the withdrawal of little-used Sunday services, or bus substitution. Any investment in rolling stock or infrastructure purely for regional services is paid for by the Region, although there is usually a significant contribution from SNCF and central government. In some cases, the investment is then paid back over a period, typically of 15 years, by SNCF.

The Brittany (Bretagne) Region signed up in 1985, when local services cost FF 180 million per year against receipts totalling FF 60 million, the difference, FF 120 million, coming from central government (a total of around FF 3,500 million is paid nationwide). Unfortunately for the Region, recent periods have seen revenue from workers' season tickets falling by 10% a year, and the Region is being forced to contribute FF 4 million per year to rail services. On the other hand, favourable circumstances left the Nord-Pas-de-Calais Region with a surplus to reinvest in 1989. The Bretagne Region has since made frequent adjustments to local services and even introduced a completely new summer tourist service from Auray to Quiberon, which has covered its costs better than most other regional services. Finally, Bretagne contributed FF 68 million between 1986 and 1990 to capital projects such as upgrading track on the Brest-Quimper line and improving station facilities. Hand-wringing by the Region over these amounts is a little difficult to take when one compares the sums with the FF 3,285 million (FF 577 from the Region) to be spent on dual carriageway roads in the Region during 1989-1993!

Anatomy of a Closure
From the summer timetable 1989, SNCF in concert with the Auvergne Region decided to close the Bort-les-Orgues — Neussargues line in the Massif Central. This was a difficult line to operate as it has several sections at between 1 in 33 and 1 in 40, plus some very tight curvature. End to end timings with the powerful X2800 single units gave an average speed of only 45km/h (28mph) and the line had receipts covering only 1/16 of operating costs with trains often running completely empty with an average of six passengers overall.

This level is not too surprising given that the area has an ageing population, the total of which fell by 18% between the last two censuses. Several stations are far from population centres and road improvements now put Bort at 1hr 20min from Clermont-Ferrand by car against 3hr 30min by train, with two changes sometimes necessary.

Bustitution of the service, with some adaptations to timings, has allowed Auvergne Region to make considerable savings, which will be used to finance a new return trip from Aurillac to Clermont-Ferrand at peak times.

REGIONAL SERVICE FINANCES 1988
Total Costs FF 6,147 million

Revenue sources	FF million	
Passenger receipts	1,770	28.8%
Social Fares Compensations	750	12.2%
Central Government	3,474	56.5%
Regional Government	55	0.9%
SNCF Funds	98	1.6%

Source: *SNCF Plan d'Enterprise 1990-1994*

THE FRENCH REGIONS

Having successfully started decentralising responsibility for local services to the Regions, and with some startling new liveries appearing on local trains — Languedoc-Roussillon plumped for orange, blue and green stripes on white — SNCF promptly put a stop to the increasing decadence in 1987 when it decided to market regional trains nationally as TER — *Trains Express Régionaux* (Regional Express Trains). Although the intention was to awake people's attention to the renaissance of local trains, and emphasising the word *Express* rather than the much maligned *Omnibus*, this move smacked of the Paris Kremlin stamping on a nascent perestroika. From then on, orange and rainbow-striped white were out and the choice of standard green, red, yellow or blue was given to the regions. SNCF's Regional Actions Manager, Jacques Chauvineau, claims that the advantages of a common image allow advertising at a national level. In addition, he suggests that a common policy is necessary to avoid 'Balkanisation', with services terminating at regional boundaries, when research shows that 20% of all TER passengers are making inter-regional journeys.

The policies of the Regions

themselves vary depending on local politics but most aim mainly to improve and adapt peak trains to cater for work and schools traffic. All Regions have aimed to improve connections with main line services, especially Paris trains and more especially TGVs. Some aim to upgrade links between major towns within the Region. Other typical aims are the *désenclavement* of the area and *aménagement du territoire* — two vague terms, which mean roughly the opening up of an isolated region such as the Massif Central and strategic planning of the territory.

Feedback from the Regions shows that their relationship with SNCF is sometimes rather uneasy. Certain Regions are happy to let SNCF get on with doing what it does best — running trains — intervening little from year to year. Picardie Region, for example, has made few changes to local timetables since taking over responsibility. Other Regions, perhaps with greater ambitions, have fallen out with SNCF over several subjects, in particular, rolling stock and service accounting. The latter is dealt with at greater length in the section on the A2E railbus.

Certain actions have been carried out by the majority of the Regions since signing agreements with SNCF. Many have financed new rolling stock and almost all have paid for the repainting of locally used rolling stock (and coaches for road services) in their chosen livery in

Above left: **EMU No 17364 is pictured at Avignon on 26 June 1989. These standardised units, of which 160 of Classes Z 7300, Z 7500, Z 9500, Z 9600, Z 11500 have been built generically known as Class Z2, were conceived for semi-fast and stopping services where their high power/weight ratio gives good acceleration.** *Jonathan Falconer*

Left: **An Alsthom-built electric locomotive of Class BB 22200, No 22252, climbs from St Cyr with train 6131, the 15.20 Marseille-Nice on 19 May 1989. By this date, SNCF had started to drop the 'BB' prefix from the locomotive number.** *Brian Stephenson.*

Above: **The Class BB 22200 are outwardly similar to the Class BB 7200 series, but unlike the latter class are dual voltage, which makes them useful all over SNCF's electrified network. Here one of the class hauls at eastbound freight for Ventimiglia over the viaduct at Antheor Cap-Roux on 23 May 1989.** *Brian Stephenson*

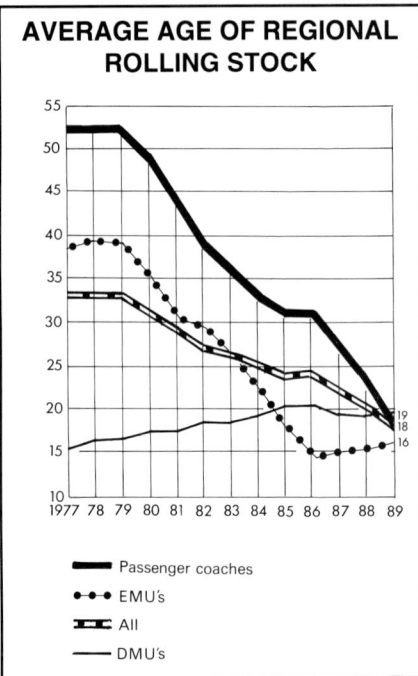

AVERAGE AGE OF REGIONAL ROLLING STOCK

— Passenger coaches
••• EMU's
⊥⊥⊥ All
— DMU's

order to publicise their role in local transport. About half have financed and published free, easy to read, local timetable guides to a common format. Some of the Regions have decided to include information about long distance trains, ferry, bus and air services as well as town plans. These guides are a marked contrast to SNCF's national timetables which are extremely expensive, difficult to obtain and very badly drafted. Ten Regions are now considering offering this information on the Minitel network. Most Regions have also introduced some sort of through ticketing facility. In most cases this has been an add-on to the usual SNCF season ticket, where the user can buy a bus season ticket for the beginning or end (or both) of his journey, at a reduced price. Multi-modal Travelcard style tickets have been rare in France, perhaps due to the plethora of bus operators in most areas and more dispersed patterns of settlement. Seven Regions with tourist potential (but surprisingly including the Nord-Pas-de-Calais) have created a special ticket in order to attract visitors to the local train services. In most cases, purchase of a special card allows unlimited 50% fares reductions during a set period.

The results of the Regions' efforts so far have varied and depended on the potential travel markets plus the Regions' ability to tap it. As mentioned, Picardie Region has changed its services very little since signing up. On the other hand Midi-Pyrénées, based around Toulouse, increased train/km by 40% from 1981 to 1989, and traffic has grown by 55%. The same Region has invested substantially in track improvements, which have allowed an increase in average train speeds to 70km/h against an average of 64km/h elsewhere. Several other Regions have followed Midi-Pyrénées' lead on track upgrades since.

The most ambitious regional plan is that of Alsace which intends to increase intra-regional express speeds to 200km/h. The Strasbourg-Mulhouse line has often been used in the past for one-off trials, and its curvature and profile are ideal for high-speed running. Thus, an investment of FF 72 million is currently being made in order to upgrade signalling, introduce automatic speed control and eliminate level crossings so that 15 minutes will be shaved off present Strasbourg-Mulhouse times of just over one hour. 40% of the finance will come from the Region, 35% from central government and 25% from the two Alsatian *départements* of Bas Rhin and Haut Rhin. Contributions towards level crossing elimination will also have come from many towns along the line. In late 1991, *Sybic* locomotives and specially adapted Corail stock will replace the 140km/h limited RRR rakes on the Strasbourg-Mulhouse-Basel line.

Problems with rolling stock were similar to those inherited by BR's Provincial Sector. Regional services in the past tended to inherit cascaded rolling stock which was unsuitable for local needs. In France, many local services were worked by stock which

Below: **The creation of 22 regional councils was one of the main spurs to the saving of many of SNCF's local services in the regions. Another factor was the introduction of push-pull services using stock such as this illustrated here in the blue/silver livery of the Provence-Alpes-Cote d'Azur region.** *SNCF.*

Bottom: **Before modernisation, No BB 66486 prepares to depart from Lille with a train of 1930s vintage coaches, originally built for the Chemin de Fer du Nord, in April 1978.** *Rail Info Collection/Jerome Koch*

was either rather old or expensive to operate. The situation is still not perfect but much improved. For instance, the average age of hauled stock fell from 52 to 18 years between 1977 and 1989. Ancient main line stock has generally been replaced by 3 or 4-car stainless steel push-pull rakes, first of the RIB then the RRR type. Although a definite advance on previous stock, with 2+2 seating and moquette seats with armrests, they remain a little spartan for longer runs and have no air-conditioning, which is a must for much of the year in southern regions. SNCF was vehemently criticised for introducing RRR stock between Marseille and Briançon, a run of nearly four hours, where trains were previously worked by Corail coaches.

The average age of EMUs also fell over the same period, from 38 to 16 years and many of the older remaining units have been modernised. Most of the EMUs on regional services are variations on the Z2 two-car unit. This 100mph design, with air conditioning and extremely fast acceleration, was introduced from 1980 as 'quality' stock for local services connecting into TGVs and on medium distance expresses such as Lyon-Geneva. Although indeed used on this type of service, they have also found their way on to many less glamorous duties, and it has been clear from SNCF and the Regions that they are far too expensive for these. And although RRR rakes are fine for large peak loads, SNCF has yet to find an EMU which combines two-car flexibility with RRR prices.

The only section of stock which has aged over the 1977-89 period is DMUs, which have risen from 15 to 18 years on average. The mainstay of SNCF's DMU fleet, which are mainly used on regional services, are the 450 ANF two-car units built between 1963 and 1981. Most of these are fitted with 2+3 plastic covered bench seats which represent a distinct turn-off these days. SNCF has proposed modernisation (modernised exterior and interior with individual seats) to the Regions and around 50 have so far been treated. However, their acceleration leaves much to be desired, and their maximum speed of 120km/h is very poor by modern standards.

The Regions, headed by the Centre, are now pressing for a new design and

Top: **After modernisation, a Class BB 66400 diesel is seen near Boulogne in push mode with a Calais-Lille train via St Pol and Bethune. The rolling stock is a newly introduced RIB push-pull three car set. The Nord-Pas-de-Calais Region's development plan for local services was one of the early successes in the provinces.** *Yves Broncard*

Left: **On 10 April 1987, Class Z 7300 1,500V dc two-car provincial EMU No 917303, in 'Transport Languedoc-Rousillon' livery, waits at Béziers with the 16.04 service to Neussargues. The livery is white with bands of orange, green and blue along the sides.** *David Brown*

Left: **With the dramatic landscape of the Alps in the background, a TGV-Sud-Est unit demonstrates the colourful grey, white and orange livery of the Sud Est service.** *SNCF.*

Below far left: **For the TGV-Atlantique a new livery of silver blue and white has been adopted. Here a rake of TGV-Atlantique stock leaves the station of Guingamp heading for Paris Montparnasse in August 1990.** *Rail Info Collection*

Below left: **The A2E Railbus, operated by the Chemins de Fer et Transports Automobiles (CFTA) in the Bretagne Region has reduced operating costs considerably. However, this is mainly due to one-man operation and not the design of the train itself.** *Rail Info Collection*

Top: **One of the A2E railbuses built for the Bretagne Region by Soule and operated on the region's behalf by CFTA** *(Chemins de Fer et Transports Automobiles)* **is seen at Carhaix, terminus of the branch line from Guingamp. This is one of two lines in the region over which these A2E units operate on an experimental basis.**
Rail Info Collection

Above: **'Bustitution' of local rail services has become increasingly common during the 1980s. Carhaix in Brittany is the point of convergence for routes from Rosporden, Loudeac and Chateaulin, with onward rail connections to Guingamp.**
Rail Info Collection

SNCF is at present drawing up specifications. They are looking for a unit which will give much improved acceleration and speed with comfort at an affordable price, given regional traffic levels. Already eyes have been cast in the direction of Derby. The search for economy is also a constant in regional preoccupations. Many have accepted the role of the coach in replacing trains on lightly used lines, but others are still looking for a rail solution at a coach price. This has led the Bretagne Region to investigate an 'economic' railbus solution, known as A2E.

The Railbus Experiment
In researching SNCF regional services, the lack of any proposal for one-man operation of rural services has been conspicuous by its absence. Local services in many areas of France, but particularly the Massif Central, are operated by single railcars manned by driver and guard, and very lightly used at most times of the week and year. It became evident from conversations with SNCF at an early stage that fear of the unions was the main reason for this. However, it seems very strange that in Paris one man (with suitable back-up technology, of course) can pilot a double-deck train crush-loaded with 1,000 commuters whereas the Bort-les-Orgues to Aurillac line continues to employ two staff for as many passengers.

So a very interesting chapter in the saga of regional services opened in 1990 with the delivery of three 'economic' two-axle railbus, known as A2E (*Autorail à 2 éssieux* — 2-axle railcar) to the Bretagne Region. This project was hatched by elements within the Bretagne Region and concerns three railbuses built by Soulé of Bagnères de Bigorre for a cost of FF 16 million, which has been shared by Central Government FF 4 million, the Region FF 4 million and CFTA FF 8 million, to be financed by loans. Of this, 4 million was spent on development and FF 12 million on construction of the three railbuses. The A2E is the result of a search for a railbus with average operating costs somewhere between those of a classic diesel railcar (FF 55/km) and a coach (FF 10/km).

The major economy to be gained from A2E operation is from dropping the guard. However, this has not been achieved through co-operation with SNCF unions. The units will be used on two lines in Brittany, Guingamp-Paimpol and Guingamp-Carhaix which have appalling operating ratios — costs were 10 times as high as receipts on Guingamp-Carhaix and five times as high on Guingamp-Paimpol in 1988. These lines, through a quirk of history, are operated by a private rail/bus company, the *Chemins de Fer et Transports Automobiles* (CFTA). On other French lines, CFTA operates freight trains with one man instead of SNCF's three.

This experiment has provoked much comment. Firstly, there is disagreement within the Bretagne Region itself over the usefulness of a unit which lacks the flexibility and comfort of a modern coach, but which cannot operate any faster on rural lines (the network of Breton lines are restricted to 70km/h) without expensive investment on track. Nor can this 'economic' unit bring costs down anywhere near that of a coach – A2E costs around 35 FF/km compared with 10 FF/km for a coach and 55 FF/km for 'Classic' railcar. It is clear that other Regions with lightly used services and SNCF itself are very interested in the results of this experiment. Another twist in this tale is the problems that the Bretagne Region has faced over judging the economic impact of the replacement of SNCF X2100 units by the new railbuses on the Carhaix and Paimpol services. The SNCF accounting system uses a national average cost per train/kilometre which does not take into account local conditions. The iniquities of such a system are manifest and make local cost management impossible. They also meant that a comparison of pre- and post-railbus costs would be impossible without an exceptional accounting system for the project. After much SNCF resistance, the Region pressed and won its case.

It remains to be seen what conclusions are to be drawn from the experiment. Operating costs per km have reduced by 40% whilst revenue has risen by around 40%. However at the same time, the rail service has been increased at the expense of the road alternative. SNCF remains deeply sceptical of the experiment. However, one point is clear: it is the removal of the guard which was responsible for the major economy. It wasn't necessary to build the A2E units to discover this!

SNCF's president, Jacques Fournier, admitted in a recent interview their methods of operation on these marginal services were 'overly cumbersome'. Whether SNCF managers will ever grasp the manning issue remains to be seen.

Paris

PASSENGER TRAFFIC (1,000 MILLION PASSENGER KM)									
1981	1982	1983	1984	1985	1986	1987	1988	1989	1990
7.50	7.67	7.97	8.20	8.47	8.61	8.65	8.91	9.13	9.31

ROLLING STOCK							
Coaching stock 1983-1989	1983			1986			1989
Modern single-deck coaches	380			504			504
Double-deck coaches	551			768			1019
Total vehicles	3,034	3,001	3,067	3,049	3,026	3,041	3,073

The administrative region of Ile-de-France, which includes Paris and its suburbs in the seven surrounding départements, covers only 2% of the land area (4,000sq km) of France but contains 18% of the country's population, with a total of around 10 million people and 4.5 million jobs. The area remains the economic heart of France, despite determined attempts at decentralisation in recent years. The city of Paris is a département in itself and has a population of approximately 2 million living in an area of only 105 sq km. This is Paris 'intra-muros' — within the boundary of the old city walls, long since gone and now followed roughly by the Boulevard Périphérique, the circular urban motorway which so many British motorists fear.

Like London, the management of the city Métro (by RATP — Régie Autonome des Transports Parisiens) is separate from that of the region's full-sized railways. These are largely run by SNCF, although most of RER Line A and the southern half of line B are run by RATP. Unlike the London Underground, which penetrates deep into the outer suburbs, the Paris Métro was constructed as a dense network of 13 lines to serve Paris 'intra-muros'. Its operation outside the city walls is minor and started only in the 1970s.

Like central London, Paris itself has lost population in recent years. Firstly, this was to the *Petite Couronne* — the inner ring of suburbs in the *départments* of Hauts-de-Seine, Seine-Saint-Denis and Val-de-Marne. During the 1980s, the trend has been for people to move even further out to the *Grande Couronne* — the outer ring of suburbs, up to 70km from the capital, in the Yvelines, Essonne, Val-d'Oise and Seine-et-Marne départments. With employment problems in more far-flung towns, people have also started to commute even further from towns such as Beauvais (78km), Amiens (131km) and even Rouen (140km).

The Ile-de-France Region is now completely covered by *La Région des Transports Parisiens* — Paris Transport Region. All public transport within the Region is supervised by a commission of 24 members, the *Syndicat des Transports Parisiens* with delegates from the city itself, the seven other *départements,* central government, local companies and users groups. As would be expected, SNCF operates high-frequency, high-capacity trains over the now entirely electrified network of Paris suburban lines. As a rule, in the off-peak, these are every 15 minutes for distances up to 15km from the centre and every half hour up to 30km. Altogether 5,000 trains a day carry 1,600,000 passengers. Traffic has increased constantly over the past 10 years at an average of 2-3% per year (see above) and is set to continue throughout the 1990s. This increase is fuelled by regular improvements to services and infrastructure together with the highly affordable *Carte Orange* season ticket (see below).

The Carte Orange
Introduced 15 years ago, the *Carte Orange* is a multi-modal travelcard covering the Ile-de-France Region. This was until recently divided into five zones (not including the southern extremities), to which three more were added in January 1991 so as to cover the whole Region. The card is now used by 2 million people, who constitute 60 to 65% of public transport users in the area. In 1990, monthly prices ranged from FF

Right: **Entering Puteaux station on a Paris St Lazare-St Cloud service a 25kV Z 6400 EMU passes the closed-circuit television monitor which allows drivers to observe passenger movements along the length of the train. Despite opposition from the unions, these units (which were introduced in 1976) were the first on SNCF to be one-man operated.** *Yves Broncard*

Above: **140km/h push-pull stock of 'RRR' type has been introduced on regional services throughout France. Here Lille-Reims and Reims-Lille afternoon services cross at Douai in August 1991. The trains are powered by the ubiquitous BB 67400 diesel-electrics, which are based at Longneau (Amiens) depot.**
Rail Info Collection

Left: **Although there is a long tradition of locomotive-hauled double-deck coaching stock on SNCF, it was only with the introduction of the Class Z 5600 EMUs in 1983 for Paris suburban services that the first double-deck multiple units appeared. The striking red, white and blue livery, evinced here by the second unit in the class No 5602, distinguishes these units from the earlier double-deck coaching stock which has a yellow and white livery.**
SNCF

173 for Zones 1 and 2 — covering Paris plus a narrow band outside its walls to FF 501 for eight zones which take you almost 100km from the centre in certain directions.

As well as large numbers of EMUs, SNCF deploys push-pull rakes of single- or double-deck stock out of all termini. All recent deliveries have been of double-deck EMUs, and Paris rolling stock now has an average age of 12 years and falling. Of note is the dominance of St Lazare, the busiest station in Europe with 380,000 passengers a day, of which 60,000 arrive between 08.00 and 09.00.

The development of SNCF services in the Paris region has mainly been within the RER system although the network is partly run by RATP. In the early 1960s came the idea of the RER (*Réseau Express Régional*) — a Regional Express Network to serve the medium and outer suburbs of Paris and, above all, the new towns which were to be built at Marne-la-Vallée, Cergy-Pontoise, St Quentin-en-Yvelines, Evry and Melun-Sénart. In contrast with the existing SNCF suburban lines with their traditional termini, the new lines would interlink via tunnels, thus penetrating to the heart of Paris. The development of the RER has been a mix of completely new construction allied to the upgrading of existing lines. Built to standard French loading gauge, the first sections all belonged to RATP, with current developments almost exclusively on SNCF terrain.

RER Line A
This was the first line to be opened (entirely RATP), in stages between 1969 and 1972, and originally was formed as a western branch from St Germain-en-Laye to Nanterre (formerly SNCF) linked via a new tunnel to an eastern branch from Vincennes to Boissy-St-Léger (formerly RATP). To this was added a completely new branch from Vincennes to Marne-la-Vallée new town (terminus

Torcy) opened in two stages in 1977 and 1980.

Line A remained in this configuration, operated by RATP units operating off 1,500V dc overhead until 1988, when the SNCF line from Nanterre Université to Cergy St Christophe was tacked on to Line A via a new link at Nanterre Prefecture. In 1989, a new branch from Maisons Laffitte to Poissy was added to the Cergy branch. As the SNCF sections are electrified at 25kV ac, dual-voltage units of type MI84 are used on services to Cergy and Poissy.

Well before these recent extensions, Line A started to suffer growing pains. From 1980, traffic grew continuously, first at 10%, then at 4-5% per year. Problems became most acute on the central section from Gare de Lyon to Auber, where passenger growth reached 90% in five years. Reliability problems were tackled with a refurbishment programme for the ageing RATP MS61 units and an unusual campaign encouraging passenger boarding/alighting discipline at crucial city centre stations, thus allowing stops to be limited to 50sec, reduced late-running from 20% to 8% during 1988. Despite this, and a 2 ½ min peak frequency, Line A was still only providing crush capacity of 44,500 passengers per hour in each direction whereas daily figures were already 50,000 and growing in 1988. My experience at Châtelet between 08.00 and 09.00 was that it was rare to be able to board the first train to arrive.

In early 1990, a decision was finally made on measures to relieve Line A and to improve access to the centre of Paris generally. The line from Châtelet to Gare de Lyon will be quadrupled in order to link the north and south sections of Line D (see below). Second is a project known as EOLE which is described below, and should drain off 17,000 passengers per hour. The third project, known as METEOR, is purely RATP and involves the construction of a small loading gauge, completely automatic, Métro line, from St Lazare to Gare de Lyon. This will siphon off 12,000 passengers per hour from the central section of Line A and will cost FF 3,300 million.

Relief for Line A will not be before time. The extensions to Cergy and Poissy are still bringing traffic increases and the prolongation of the Torcy branch to EuroDisneyland (and its future TGV station) will certainly put further pressure on services. In the meantime, a shorter term solution to Line A's woes was necessary. During 1989, an automatic driving system called SACEM (*Système de l'aide à la Conduite, l'Exploitation et le Maintenance*) was introduced at a cost of FF 650 million. Basically this system overrides the conventional signalling system over the central section of Line A during peak periods, allowing headways to reduce to two minutes. This increases the line's capacity to 54,000 per hour. It has now been decided to operate double-deck units as this would allow a 19% increase in capacity, and a prototype bi-level coach with three doors was incorporated in an MS61 unit from January 1991. If loading/unloading trials are successful, this type of stock will become standard for RATP/SNCF in future.

RER Line B

Line B was formed by connecting the SNCF line from Gare du Nord to Mitry, and its new branch from Aulnay to Roissy (Charles de Gaulle) airport, to the former RATP Sceaux line from Luxembourg to St Rémy-les-Chevreuse and its branch to Robinson. The Sceaux line was first extended northwards to Châtelet in 1977, allowing interchange with Line A. In 1981 trains were again extended to Gare du Nord, where RATP 1,500V dc now meets SNCF 25kV ac, and RATP and SNCF crews change over. From 1981 to 1985, as MI79 dual-voltage units were delivered, services were gradually interconnected until 20 through trains per hour were being operated in the peak. In February 1988

Above: **Despite the introduction of large numbers of double-deck EMUs, many Paris suburban services are still operated by push-pull stock. Here a Class BB 17000 electric locomotive propels a Creil-Paris Nord working out of Orryla-Ville in May 1991.** *Rail Info Collection*

St-Michel station opened, allowing interchange with RER Line C as well as Métro lines 4 and 10. St Michel is now the second hub of the RER system, after Châtelet where Lines A, B and D interconnect. The massive cost of the station — around £45 million at 1988 prices — is justified by the its use by 30 million passengers per year.

Significant future developments on the line include the opening of Massy-Palaiseau TGV station on the Atlantique line in September 1991, plus the construction of a VAL-type (similar to that in Lille) automatic metro from Antony station to Orly airport, which will open in October 1991. Although this will bring further traffic to the RER, SNCF would have preferred their project of serving Orly by building a branch off Line C (see below). At the other end of the line, a one kilometre extension will improve penetration of Roissy airport.

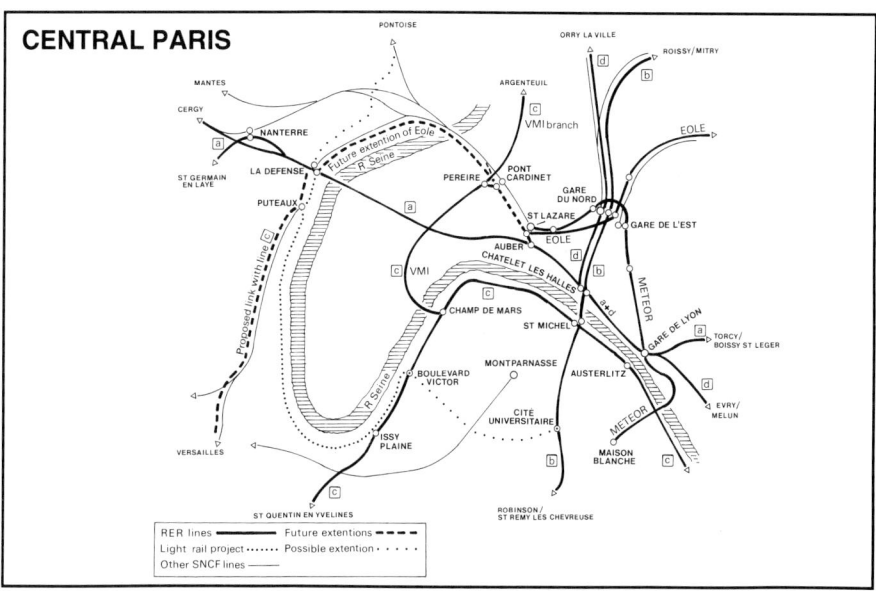

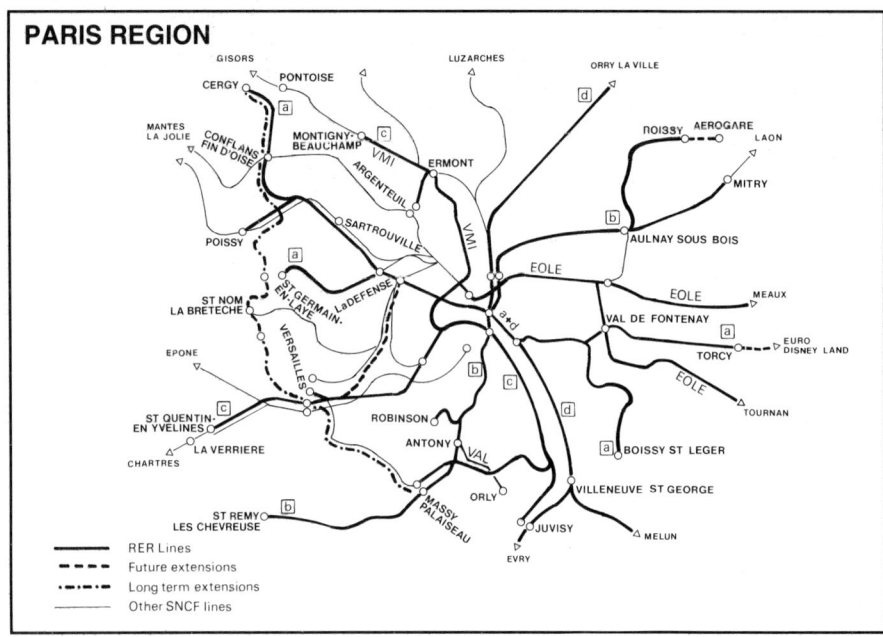

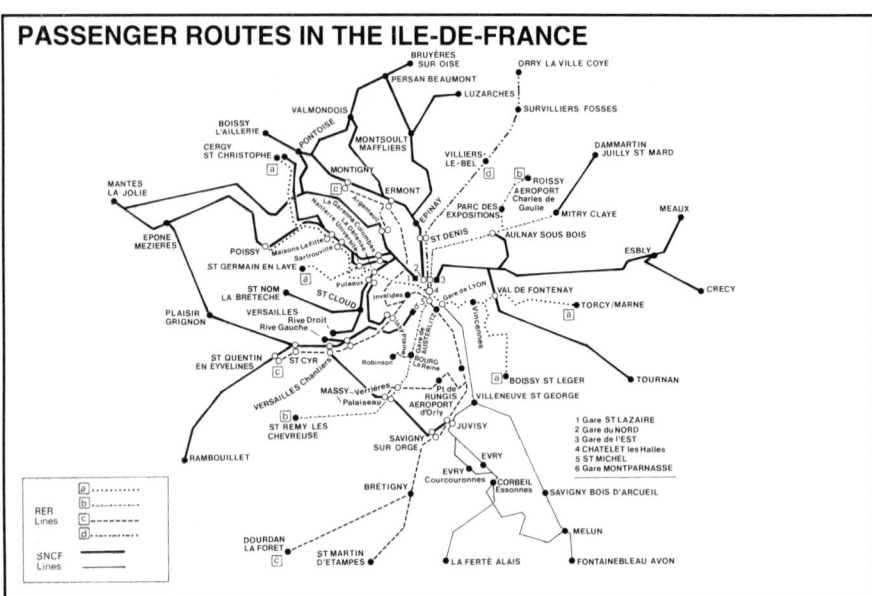

Line C

RER Line C was the first to be operated entirely by SNCF, and opened in 1980. Originally, services from the south ran along the left bank of the Seine from Austerlitz to Quai d'Orsay. Trains from Versailles in the west terminated at Invalides, only half a mile away. By linking the two lines, Line C became by far the cheapest RER creation, but provided many new through links and interchange possibilities with the Métro.

Developments continue apace on Line C. In 1988 a new branch from Champ-de-Mars to the northwestern suburbs of Argenteuil and Montigny was opened. Unfortunately, the story of VMI was pretty disastrous. What started as a low-cost plan to re-use several closed or poorly-appointed SNCF lines became compromised by environmental demands pushing the line underground in several areas. SNCF did not have the Channel Tunnel link cop-out of 'no public money', and the bill grew from FF 650 million in 1980 to FF 1,871 million in 1987, and this did not even include the cost of rolling stock, a contribution of FF 275 million from the city of Paris for covering parts of the line, or add-ons such as a new station at Gennevilliers. Traffic is now reasonable, but never likely to reach the levels on Lines A and B, given the dog-leg configuration of the line.

RER Line D

Line D should have been completed some time ago but fell victim to the success of Line A. The latter's saturation has meant that the original plan to link the northern and southeastern suburbs via Line A tracks between Châtelet and Gare de Lyon was abandoned in the mid-1980s. Studies of what to do instead became inextricably tangled up with the fate of Line A, and put the decision off until the end of the decade. The Parisian Transport Syndicate finally approved a second pair of tunnels in early 1990. When opened in 1995, the 2.5km link, which will cost FF 1.55 billion, will allow through trains from Orry-la-Ville, on the Paris Nord-Creil line to Melun or La Ferté-Alais via Juvisy or Villeneuve-St Georges. The new line will be run entirely by SNCF, using dual-voltage Z20500 double-deck units.

The new line lies within one kilometre of over 15% of the Ile-de-France population, and in particular will serve Evry and Melun-Sénart new towns, which are expected to double in population during the years it takes to build the interconnection. Traffic is expected to reach 38 million passengers annually, once a fully interconnecting service of 16

Left: **At Lieusaint the LGV** *(Ligne à Grande Vitesse)* **passes over the suburban Paris network. A suburban double-deck unit passes under the flyover as a TGV working heads towards Paris.** *SNCF*

Right: **With the familiar sight of the Eiffel Tower in the background, Class Z 5300 1,500V dc four-car EMUs Nos 5440 and 5403 are seen on 4 April 1987 between Champ-de-Mars and Javel on RER Line C.** *David Brown*

Below right: **Known as 'MI79' stock, the Class Z 8100 series of dual-voltage EMUs were built between 1980 and 1984 for use on the Paris 'Interconnection' and are jointly owned by RER and SNCF. One of the class, No 8261, named *Mitry-Mory*, leaves Denfert Rochereau with a northbound service on RER Line B on 12 November 1985.** *David Brown*

peak trains per hour is operating. Line D should relieve Line A of 12,000 passengers per hour in the peaks.

The EOLE Project
EOLE which stands for *Est-Ouest Liaison Express* — East-West Express Link, is a plan under which certain services to the Gare de l'Est will be extended to St Lazare via a new tunnel, with intermediate stations at La Villette science park and a joint Est/Nord station under the RER Line B station at the Gare du Nord. This link costing FF 3,600 million was approved in 1990 and is expected to drain up to 17,000 passengers per hour from Line A. An extension of the tunnel from St Lazare to Pont Cardinet costing FF 1,700 million, has now been given the go-ahead for completion in 1997 and will be linked to the St Lazare suburban lines to Versailles and St-Nom-la-Bretèche, thus creating a new east-west link serving both La Défense and the St Lazare tertiary district.

Orbital Lines
The expansion of the Paris region has led to an increasing decentralisation of housing and employment and thus a much more varied pattern of journey making. The dispersal of these journeys makes them difficult to carry out by public transport. So whereas over half of all journeys between suburbs and Paris 'intra-muros' are made by public transport, the figure is only 14% for inter-suburban journeys. A number of proposals have recently been made public to improve orbital links, including tramways, metros, automatic or otherwise, and reserved right-of-way bus services. While these do not fall within the scope of this book, certain plans concern SNCF rail lines.

Under construction at present are flyovers at Porchefontaine/Viroflay near Versailles which will allow a direct service between St Quentin-en-Yvelines new town and La Défense. The total infrastructure investment is FF 435 million to which must be added FF 273 million for double-deck rolling stock. The service will start in 1994 and will later be extended from St Quentin to Rambouillet.

To the west of the capital, a long-term plan exists to create an orbital line linking Cergy-Pontoise new town with Massy. At present an RER interchange between Lines B and C, Massy will become a TGV station on the Atlantique line from 1991. The new orbital will be created by linking the Cergy-Achères along the 'Grand Ceinture' (GC) freight line to Versailles via St-Germain-en-Laye line, then extending to Massy via the Versailles-Massy branch. A start was made in 1990 with approval for the reopening of the GC from Noisy-le-Roi to St Germain-en-Laye in 1994, with connections to St Lazare services at St-Nom-la-Bretèche. This will involve upgrading track and electrification. Another (extremely expensive) project for the reopening of the northern part of the GC between Achères and Val-de-Fontenay was discussed during the mid-1980s, but has been shelved for the present.

Upgrading of existing infrastructure is also the aim for the Issy-Plaine-Puteaux line which is the last vestige of a once extensive 750V dc third-rail system to the west of Paris. Re-electrification and linkage to RER Line C has now been rejected in favour of a project to create a tram line from La Défense to Boulevard Victor. This could later be extended

Right: **On 6 April 1987, Class Z 8800 (Z2N) double-deck dual-voltage EMUs Nos 8833 and 8834 are seen at Ivry-sur-Seine with the 14.32 Boulevard Victor-Aeroport d'Orly service on RER line C.** *David Brown*

westwards via the *Petite Ceinture* freight line at least as far as Cité Universitaire on Line B. Northbound, the line could be extended to Argenteuil and Ermont.

Airport Links

Surprisingly, for a city which has often been praised for its public transport, Paris has really made a mess of serving its airports. In theory, Roissy in the north is served by Line B, whilst Orly in the south by Line C. The two connect at St-Michel. However, what could have been a marvellous service has been ruined by a lack of vision.

Roissy gained a rail link in 1976, when a branch was built from the Gare du Nord-Soissons line. However, the new line does not properly serve the terminal buildings and a shuttle bus is necessary for all passengers. This has been found to be a turn-off and the rail service has never carried the expected number of passengers. It seems that this wrong will be righted by 1994 as approval has now been won to extend Line B one kilometre to a new terminus between Terminals 1 and 2, from which a people mover system will distribute passengers. The new RER terminus will also interchange with the TGV Interconnexion line.

Orly started to be served by a regular interval service out of Austerlitz low-level in 1972. For this, part of the *Grande Ceinture* circular freight line was reopened. However, that was as far as it went, and passengers are still detrained at Pont de Rungis and shuttled to the airport by bus. Usage has been so disappointing that the original Orly semi-fast trains were downgraded to all-stations. The cost of a proposed spur into the airport was considered too expensive in 1972, and a proposal for a similar chord was rejected in 1988 in favour of an automatic metro, similar to that in Lille, from Antony station on Line B.

Finance

Readers with calculators will perhaps be gasping once they tot up the total investment in the RER system over the next five years (not including any major, but routine track renewal), which in fact will total FF 15.7 billion (£1.57 billion).

In general, 40% of this comes from central government, either in budget credits or via the *versement de transport*. This is a tax on all companies employing 10 people or more, which is used directly for public transport. Normally 1% of payroll, it has been raised to 1.75% in Paris recently, as well as in other cities investing in rapid transit schemes. Another 40% of the bill come from the Ile-de-France Region out of local taxes on households, with the final 20% coming in loans to SNCF (or RATP) from the Region.

In certain cases, where a project has an impact on a particular *département,* the latter may contribute, from its own budget, with revenue drawn from local taxes. An example is the St Quentin-en-Yvelines to La Défense link which benefits the Yvelines *département.* Special cases exist such as the extension of Line B within Roissy airport. Of the FF 545 million (for one kilometre plus a station!) 36% is from the Region, 54% from a loan to be repaid from airport surcharges, and 10% from SNCF and the Paris airports authority.

As far as operating costs are concerned, passenger fares finance only 35% of the total, with the rest coming from taxes raised by central government and the Ile-de-France Region and *départements* (17%) and most importantly from the *versement de transport* which provides 40% of the total. The subsidy goes mainly to keep commuting costs down through the extremely affordable *Carte Orange* season tickets.

INVESTMENT IN FF MILLION (CONSTANT VALUE)							
	1983	1984	1985	1986	1987	1988	1989
Renewal	647	873	1065	1047	874	729	779
Network extension	213	311	370	334	350	599	623
Total investment	860	1,184	1,435	1,381	1,224	1,328	1,402

PARIS SUBURBAN FINANCES 1988		
Revenue sources	FF million	
Passenger receipts	2,050	34.8%
Employers' Carte Orange refund	495	8.4%
'Social' Fares Compensations	2,344	39.8%
Central Government*	701	11.9%
Local Government*	300	5.1%

Total costs: FF 5,890 million

*These two make up the Indemnité Compensatrice Banlieue

Source: SNCF Plan d'Enterprise 1990-1994

Left: **Two asynchronous-motored dual-voltage double-deck EMUs of Class Z 20500 arrive at Les Noues with an Orry-la-Ville-Chatelet service on RER line D in May 1991.** *Rail Info Collection*

Freight

Freight carried by SNCF is somewhat different from that which is hauled in Britain — see Table 1. Firstly, much less coal is transported, as France has few remaining deposits and 80% of power is generated by nuclear power stations. Secondly, SNCF carries far more food/agricultural produce than BR — for example, mineral water, wine and cereals. In general, because of the spread of settlement, hauls are much longer — Table 1 shows that average haul length for inter-modal traffic, which is targeted for future growth is almost 600km. This is a trend which is likely to continue in future as management concentrates on profitable flows between France's large conurbations and on international traffic.

Like most European rail authorities, the amount of freight carried by SNCF has been in almost continuous decline in recent years, in absolute terms. Since the first oil crisis in 1973, traffic has fallen by one-third from 74 billion to 50.6 billion tonne km in 1988. Recent stabilisation has not stopped loss of market share, with road transport making continuous gains at rail's expense — see Table 3. In 10 years, SNCF has seen its traffic fall by 20% from 64.8 billion tonne km in 1980 to 51.6 billion in 1989. In just the last five years market share has dropped from 30% to 25.5%. Despite this, SNCF still commands the largest freight market share of the European railways.

TABLE 1: FREIGHT TRAFFIC BY COMMODITY

Traffic Type	1987 Million Tonnes	1987 Billion Tonne km	1988 Million Tonnes	1988 Billion Tonne km	1989 Million Tonnes	1989 Billion Tonne km
Inter-Modal	11.3	6.78	11.9	7.17	12.5	7.43
Steel Products & Raw Materials	29.0	7.46	30.5	8.00	31.2	8.34
Chemicals & Fertilisers	18.7	7.44	17.8	6.95	17.6	6.98
Cereals	15.0	5.55	15.1	5.60	14.9	5.64
Aggregates	17.4	5.01	19.9	5.55	20.2	5.61
Drinks	6.3	3.32	6.4	3.31	6.7	3.42
Coal	13.1	2.57	11.4	2.34	11.8	2.49
Vehicles	3.7	2.10	3.8	2.14	3.9	2.22
Other	14.3	6.29	14.2	6.27	13.8	6.00

Source: SNCF Annual Report 1989

TABLE 2: FREIGHT PERFORMANCE SINCE 1984

	1984	1985	1986	1987	1988	1989	1990	Change
Tonnes (million)	177	162	146	142	145	147	142	-20%
Tonne/km (billions)	58.4	55.8	51.7	51.3	52.3	53.3	51.5	-12%
Average haul (km)	330	344	354	361	361	363	363	+10%
Receipts (FF million)	15,230	15,498	14,565	14,115	13,868	14,093	13.574	-11%

Source: SNCF Annual Reports

TABLE 3: FRENCH INTERNAL FREIGHT TRAFFIC MODAL SPLIT

	1981	1982	1983	1984	1985	1986	1987	1988
Rail	59.8 (32.5%)	56.8	55.1	55.9	54.2	50.2	49.8	50.5 (25.8%)
Road	113.3 (61.5%)	111.2	108.1	110.3	112.0	116.6	124.5	137.9 (70.5%)
Canal	11.1 (6.0%)	10.2	9.4	8.9	8.4	7.8	7.4	7.3 (3.7%)
Total	184.2	178.2	172.6	175.1	174.6	174.6	181.7	195.7

Source: SNCF Annual Reports All figures in billion tonne km

Falling traffic has principally been due to the decline in the coal and steel industries, which have traditionally used rail. However, rail's poor performance, at a time of overall growth in freight traffic, cannot be totally linked to this factor. It has also been a consequence of poor quality and a lack of flexibility.

The effect of road competition has also forced down rail freight turnover. Road freight rates fell by 5.2% in 1987 and 5.9% in 1988, and rail has had to follow suit, eating up all SNCF's hard won productivity gains. The future does not bode well, with important extensions to the French motorway network programmed over the next 15 years, together with the 1993 deregulation of road haulage in Europe which will allow non-national hauliers to work within France. The prospect of *cabotage*, which will mean even lower rates is even making French road hauliers nervous and is sure to make road even more price competitive. However, as the recent dramatic growth of air traffic has led to congestion, this growth in lorry traffic could be a double-edged sword.

Left: **Grain traffic has been a source of freight growth in recent years. Here a train of empty 'Transcereales' hoppers heads south through Arras in September 1990 behind No BB 16541, with a Class BB 25500 in tow.** *Rail Info Collection/Ernest Godward*

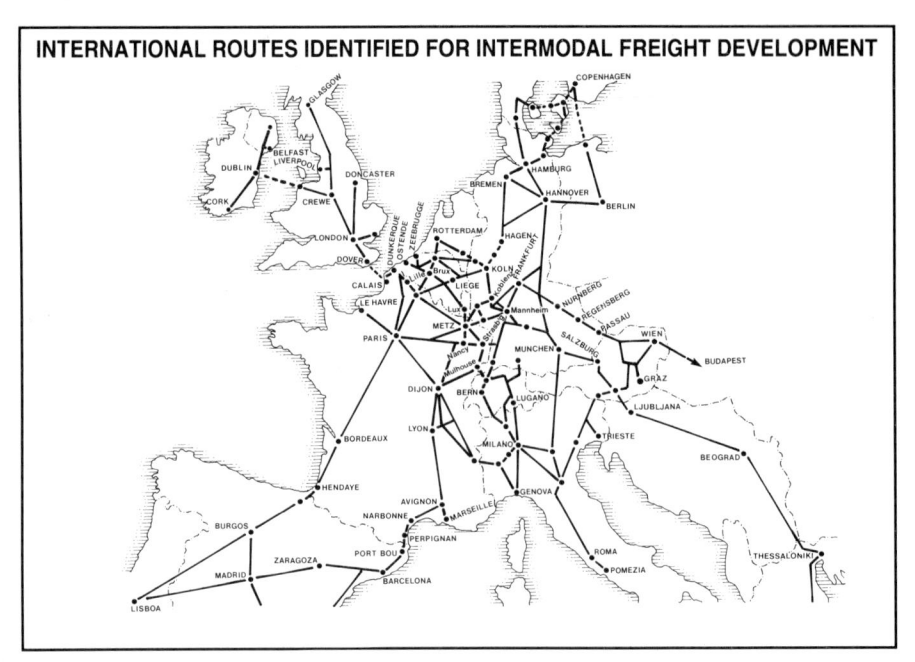

INTERNATIONAL ROUTES IDENTIFIED FOR INTERMODAL FREIGHT DEVELOPMENT

There was a 50% increase in heavy lorries on motorways within two years at the tail end of the 1980s, a trend which is sure to bring congestion and help SNCF in the longer term.

SNCF management have become increasingly hard-nosed in recent times in facing up to this competition, and this has led to a three-pronged attack through cost reduction, increases in overall transit speeds and quality improvements. Fret SNCF does not specify how much its services lose at present, but hopes to balance its books by the end of the decade with a turnover of FF 13.2 billion, and to stabilise its traffic at 52 billion tonne km. However, 1990 started badly — traffic fell by 3% to around 51.5 million tonne km due to the general recession and quality problems centring on shortages of drivers and traction.

However, there are opportunities to be grasped, particularly in international traffic. The opening of the Channel Tunnel in 1993 is expected to allow a significant traffic gain, and the abolition of EC frontier formalities in the same year should allow productivity gains and faster international transits. SNCF is not gambling on it, but environmental pressures may also lead to an increased transfer to rail of complete lorries or parts thereof in one of the many intermodal techniques being developed at present.

When SNCF managers express serious concern about the state of freight, they are talking principally of wagonload services. Block trains make a positive contribution to finances, whilst intermodal services break even but promise much better in future. For almost 50 years, from its creation in 1938 until 1987, SNCF transported wagonload freight in separate fast (*Régime Accélérée* — RA) — and slow trains (*Régime Ordinaire* — RO). As already mentioned, there has been a continual haemorrhage of freight traffic in recent years, partly due to a decline in traditional traffics, but also because of slow management response to changing customer expectations and market opportunities.

In the mid 1980s, SNCF decided to reorganise the wagonload system in a project called ETNA (*Evolution Technologique pour un Nouvel Acheminement* — new transit through technical innovation) to take advantage of information technology and an increase in train speeds. The existing system had become outdated and costly — in many cases the two Régimes had separate yards in the same city with spare capacity in both, half empty trunk trains and connecting trip freights duplicating each other. Furthermore, the increasing demand for faster services was not being met.

The first factor in the transformation was the introduction of a real-time wagon tracing system known as NAW (*Nouvel Acheminement Wagons*) which superseded SNCF's earlier unwieldy computer system GCTM (*Gestion Centralisée du Trafic Marchandises*). The French have lagged well behind BR in this field. When TOPS was introduced in Britain in the mid-1970s, SNCF criticised the British for buying an off-the-peg American system and later decided to develop its own. This took over 10 years and seriously delayed the opportunity to make productivity gains.

The second factor was the increase in freight wagon speeds to 100km/h (62mph) throughout Europe, which allowed SNCF to abolish the division between RO and RA and create a single *Régime*, within which there is a more diversified service. Thus, classic wagonload traffic is carried in the same trains at 100km/h, but three levels of service are offered to the customer (the intermediate level is soon to be abolished), the difference being the priority given to wagons:

FRETEXPRESS : top priority with the fastest transit possible — day A/day B where distances allow
FRETRAPIDE : a slightly lower priority than FRET EXPRESS
FRETECO : a slower service at a very competitive price

An even faster service by intermodal trains running at 120, 140 or 160km/h,

RA/RO TRAFFIC SPLIT
Tonne km (billions)

	RA	RO	Total
1975	10.1	28.9	39.0
1985	15.4	16.8	32.2

Below: **The 1,500V dc Class BB 9200, introduced in 1957 and built by Schneider Jeumont, was one of the standard SNCF express passenger designs of that era. One of the class, No 9208, passes Beziers on more mundane duty, hauling a block train of hoppers.** Rail Info Collection

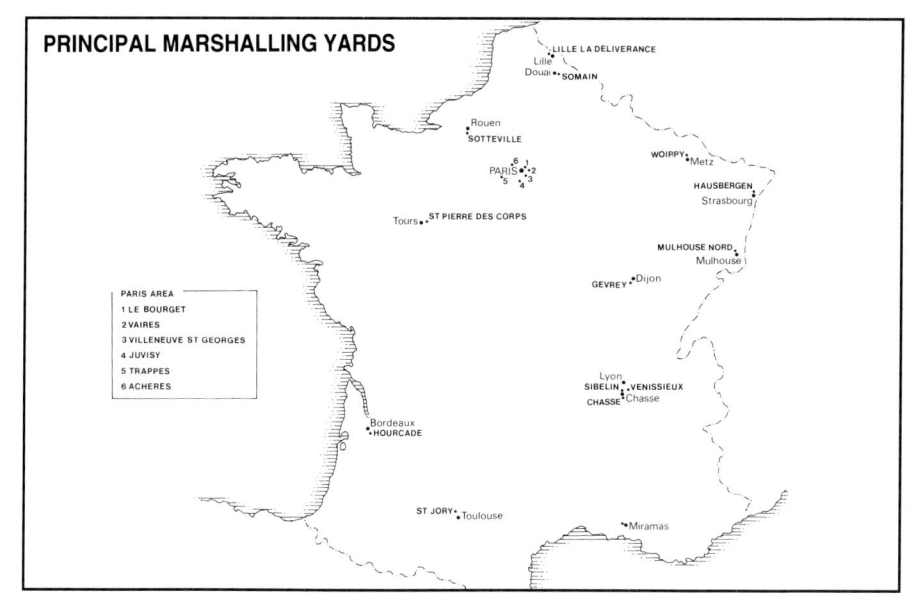

PRINCIPAL MARSHALLING YARDS

PARIS AREA
1 LE BOURGET
2 VAIRES
3 VILLENEUVE ST GEORGES
4 JUVISY
5 TRAPPES
6 ACHERES

Lille, LILLE LA DELIVERANCE, Douai, SOMAIN, Rouen, SOTTEVILLE, PARIS, WOIPPY, Metz, HAUSBERGEN, Strasbourg, Tours, ST PIERRE DES CORPS, MULHOUSE NORD, Mulhouse, GEVREY, Dijon, Lyon, SIBELIN, VENISSIEUX, CHASSE, Chasse, Bordeaux, HOURCADE, ST JORY, Toulouse, Miramas

FREIGHT TRAFFIC BY CATEGORY
Tonne-kilometres (billion)

	1978	1983	1988
Block trains	23.5	23.2	24.0
Intermodal	5.1	6.1	7.2
Wagonload	35.8	27.4	21.1
Total:	64.4	56.7	52.3

organised outside the wagonload network is called FRETCHRONO.

The abolition of the RO/RA segregation meant that locomotive performance could be fully utilised on longer, heavier trains, in general over longer distances, with less need to remarshal en route. This led quickly to better locomotive and driver productivity.

By transmitting full information about incoming services, ETNA allows train planners to know much earlier whether a scheduled trunk freight to a certain destination will be full and if a duplicate conditional *facultatif* train will have to be organised. The existence of the three levels of priority allows a certain ironing out of peaks through a reduction in these conditional workings which are always more costly to run than scheduled trains. For example, if the daily Lille-Miramas freight is full, the overflow of non urgent FRETECO wagons will be held back until the next day's working, or sent forward in another freight to the nearest destination, for example, Sibelin (Lyon) or Gevrey (Dijon), which can then forward the wagon in their next available train.

With ETNA in place, SNCF is now making attempts to improve the productivity of its 97,000 wagons. Although the 65,000 private owner wagons working in France, which are often specialised for a specific traffic, are well managed, SNCF's own fleet only manage a paltry 25 loaded trips per year spending 56% of journeys running empty. In order to to improve this lamentable situation, SNCF is introducing a computer data bank on the wagon fleet, known as MARS (*Moyens d'améliorer la répartition et séjours des wagons* — method for improving wagon allocation and layover) which should allow much more efficient utilisation of the fleet. The investment of FF 140 million should be paid back in only two years as it will save FF 90 million annually through the reduction of staff levels, wagon numbers and even train km through reduced empty running.

However, despite the savings made through ETNA, estimated at FF 600 million a year for a one-off investment of FF 1,000 million, wagonload is still in a bad way. In 1989 wagonload represented 50% of freight turnover but lost FF 1.5 billion. The present organisation of wagonload is also the source for Fret SNCF's preoccupations: remarshalling is responsible for much of the damage to goods in transit — this cost SNCF FF 44 million in 1989 and was responsible for 80% of customer complaints. Marshalling also takes far too much time in a world where SNCF is competing with road transporters which offer 24hr transits over most of France. SNCF's predictions suggest that, because of road competition forcing down rates, plus traffic transferring to intermodal trains, wagonload could be losing FF 2.3 billion a year by 1995. So, in its last five-year plan, SNCF has set out its intention of reducing wagonload to only 25% of total traffic against 35% in 1988. This will be done by the expansion of intermodal traffic from 14% to 25% and transfer to block trains.

Wagonload's problems are mainly due to having to serve too many stations on too many terminal branches. France still has a very large network of freight-only branches and 3,550 freight stations. However, only 400 of these generate 80% of present traffic, and 2,000 of them are responsible for only 2% of revenue. As well as costing much more than the revenue on offer, serving each station delays other traffic and makes fast transit impossible. SNCF's own research has shown that 85% of freight transits in France are made in 24 hours or less. In order to approach this sort of performance, it is delivery and collection of wagons which must be improved as trunk hauls between yards now show little potential for speed increase. By reducing the number of terminals serviced to around 1,200, SNCF hopes to kill the two birds of cost and speed with the same stone. Wagonload services will thus aim for a guaranteed Day A/Day C morning journey time with intermodal services covering the faster overnight transits.

In many cases collection and final delivery will be transferred to road vehicles serving one of the remaining stations. This has come to be known as FERCAMisation — FERCAM (*Chemin de FER/CAMion*) is the trading name of the road haulage part of the 83%-owned SNCF subsidiary SCETA. (Thus the operation stays within the SNCF group and, hopefully, adds a positive revenue contribution.) For example, the area around Paray-le-Monial (between Lyon and Dijon) has recently been FERCAMised. Previously, two branches to Iguérande (35km) and Charolles (15km) were served by four return trip freights on average per week. Serving the two branches would take three men a complete shift. In continual decline, traffic on the two lines was only 6,060 tonnes in 1986, the equivalent of about one wagon per working day. SNCF was therefore unsurprised to learn that final delivery by lorry would cost 90% less than by rail. The savings made from conversion have not simply been pocketed by SNCF. Instead, some has been reinvested in handling and storage facilities at Paray-le-Monial GMF (*Gare Multi-Fonction* — Multi-purpose station) in order to offer a fuller logistical package. The new product has clearly satisfied customers as traffic in the area around the Charolles branch rose from 2,660 to 3,220 tonnes in the year following conversion.

SNCF's 1990-1994 plan sees a further rationalisation of these stations as necessary. The aim is to cover France from 20 main marshalling yards, each serving 10-20 stations known as GPFs (*Gare Principal Fret*). Thus the majority of wagonload freight will be concentrated on around 300 GPFs.

FERCAMisation is now in full swing — in 1990, branch and station closures saved FF 350 million, and 600,000 tonnes of freight had to find another mode of transit. Past experience has shown that about one-third is lost completely, one-third is maintained by SNCF group lorry and another third transferred to other stations in the same catchment area. Closures have taken

INTERMODAL TERMINALS

PARIS
1 GENNEVILLIERS ♦
2 LA CHAPELLE ■
3 NOISY ●
4 VALENTON ■
5 POMPADOUR ●
6 RUNGIS ●

OPERATORS
■ CNC
● NOVATRANS
♦ CNC/NOVATRANS
▲ PRIVATE

DIRECT INTERNATIONAL FREIGHT SERVICES

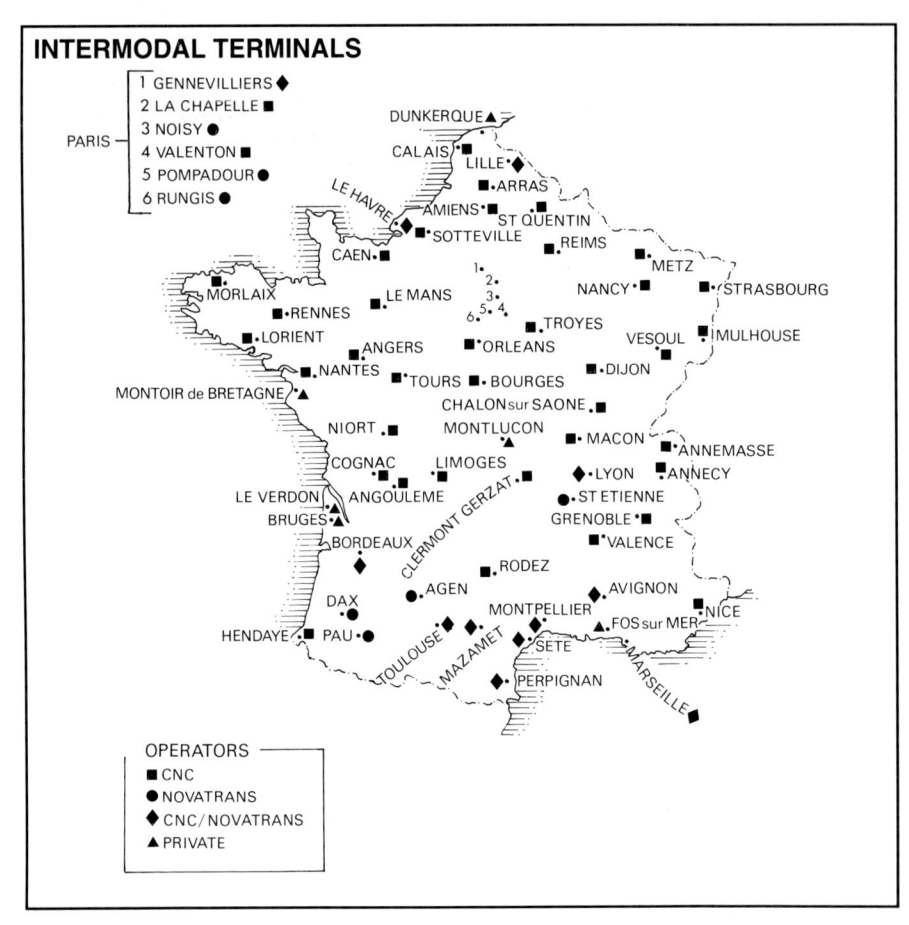

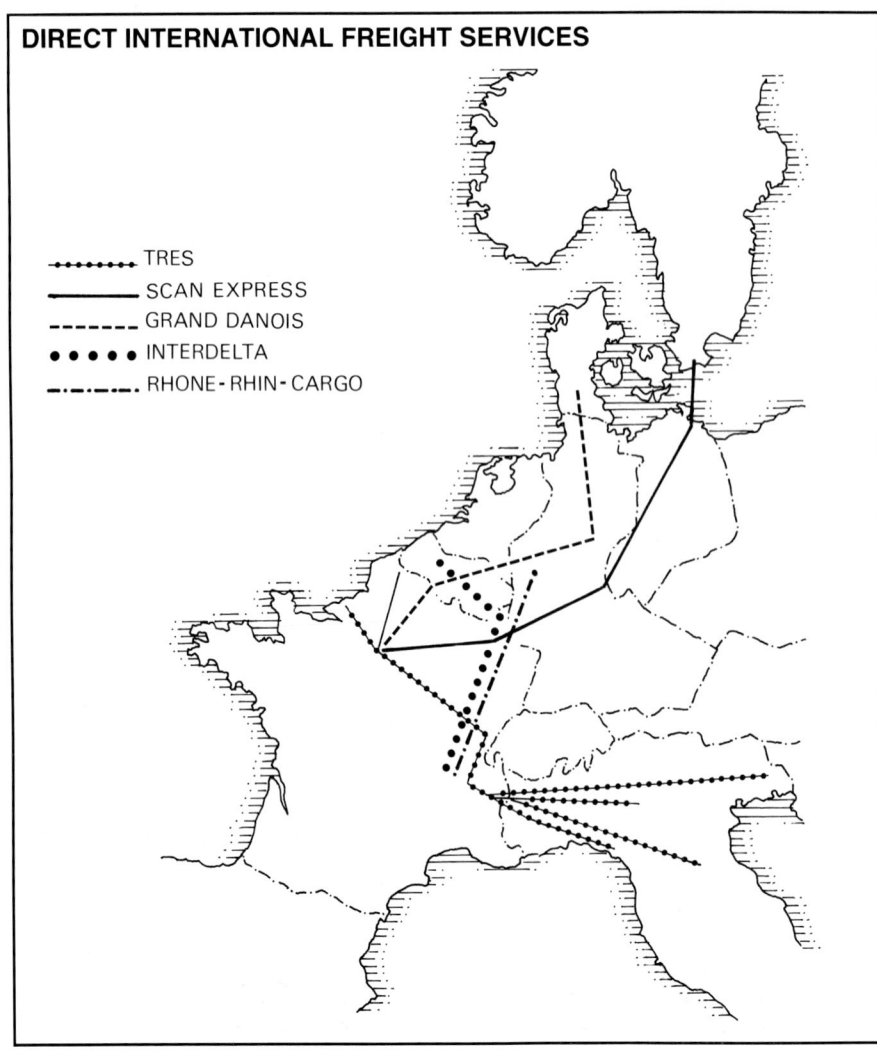

•••••• TRES
——— SCAN EXPRESS
------ GRAND DANOIS
••••• INTERDELTA
–·–·– RHONE-RHIN-CARGO

place only after a drawn out fight in many areas. In particular, politicians in Brittany, where perhaps half the freight-only branches have closed, fought tooth and nail to retain what were rather symbolic links.

Of course, transferring part of a rail freight journey to road always brings the risk that the customer will find it more attractive to avoid the cost in terms of time and money, and the risk of damage in transhipment, by using a lorry for the whole journey. In this case, SNCF hopes to win at least a part of the traffic by offering the attraction of speed. However hard a lorry driver puts his foot down (and in France they are theoretically restricted to 80km/h), it is impossible to beat the overnight transit times offered by the rapidly expanding FRETCHRONO network — the 1,000km separating Lille and Avignon is covered in 8 ½ hours at an average of 118km/h by SNCF's first 160km/h freight service.

As well as attacking terminal station and branch costs as well as delays, SNCF is looking to reduce remarshalling to a minimum by seeking 'communities of interest' within total wagonload traffic. Thus in 1989, carriage of cars was completely rethought and relaunched under the title *Formule Auto*. Whereas previously those cars produced in France or imported and not carried in block trains were treated separately, *Formule Auto* brought 60% of wagonload flows into one network, concentrated on the western Paris yard of Achères. Much of the remainder is handled at Mulhouse. Although certain routings are now longer, a specialised timetable of trains, improved surveillance plus staff specialising in the movement of cars, has led to reduced transit times and much reduced risks of damage. Concentration of wagons on a small number of sites has also facilitated the supply of empties at short notice when demanded. Economies have also been possible, due to closure of other yards.

Surprisingly, SNCF has recently been selling improvements in service based on *reductions* in freight train frequency. In the past, it has been standard practice to offer a daily service wherever possible. However, many of the services would only be to the next major yard, where long distance traffic would be remarshalled with consequent delay. Fret SNCF is now experimenting with reduction of the daily frequency on certain routes, but with radically increasing transit speeds permitting Day A evening/Day B or Day C morning transits. Thus Brittany (via Rennes yard) now has 15 daily services to the centre and east of France, plus seven trains which run two or three days a week. On the latter, customers must reserve their places in the train in order that SNCF can guarantee transit for the freight forwarded. The Bordeaux/Toulouse

Left: **Originally built as mixed traffic locomotives for the electrification of the Nord and Est regions, the Class BB 12000 has been largely relegated to freight services with the introduction of Classes BB 15000 and BB 16000. No BB 12101 propels a train of covered wagons into Sollac steel mill at Biache St Vaast, near Arras.** *Rail Info Collection*

Below left: **Increasing intermodal freight traffic (traffic up by 50% in the 10 years from 1978 to 1988) is part of SNCF's strategy to improve its freight business and SNCF has been experimenting with bi-modal techniques. A trailer designed for bimodal use is seen on test at Douai during 1991. The bogie nearest the camera replaces the lorry tractor unit when operating over the railway network. At the far end of the trailer, the three rubber-tyred axles are raised to clear the track.** *Rail Info Collection*

areas are served Tuesday, Thursday and Friday whilst Lyon and the Alps have a direct train on Monday, Wednesday and Friday.

As already mentioned, SNCF intends to reduce wagonload traffic from 35% of rail freight traffic to 25% by 1995. Most of this traffic is intended to be retained, but carried in intermodal or block trains.

Intermodal

Intermodal services will spearhead the SNCF effort to win new traffic in the 1990s. FF 1.5 billion is to be invested in intermodal techniques between 1990 and 1994 with the aim of doubling this type of traffic to 15 billion tonne km, which will take it from 15% to 25% of total freight traffic. Much of this traffic will be international-European intermodal traffic and is predicted to triple by 2005.

Intermodal services of several kinds have been around for some time on SNCF, previously being part of *Régime Accélérée* services. They included *kangarou* services, where a complete lorry trailer is carried on a low-slung wagon with pouches to take the wheel set. One such service is between Dunkerque ferry port and northern Italy. Container services are also a classic component of intermodal services. The port of Le Havre is particularly important for containers — other European traffic, some transiting via France, tends to pass via Antwerp or Rotterdam. Recently swap bodies have become increasingly popular. In response to this demand, SNCF designed its Multifret wagon — a very low bogie flat which can take swap bodies or containers and used at up to 160km/h. A number of these were hired by British Rail in 1990 in order to inaugurate swap body services between Harwich and Glasgow thus gaining experience of the technique before the opening of the Channel Tunnel.

As the 1990s opened, SNCF was beginning experiments with bimodal techniques — like the British Trailertrain system, where a lorry trailer is mounted on bogies for a rail trunk haul. A first service, initially twice weekly and with only three trailers, with a system called SemiRail (sold by ANF/Fruehauf/Remafer) began in April 1990 between Lyon and Lille. This was destined to be followed later in 1990 by a second trial between Paris and Provence with a competing system — RoadRailer (sold by AFR/Trouillet/CNC), which is licensed from the USA. A third French competitor was also waiting in the wings. However, despite the plethora of designs (the Germans, Italians and, of course, British have their own systems) it remains to be seen whether bimodal systems will find a niche market with operators.

The evolution of intermodal services is now resembling that of the TGV network. Piecemeal development is now giving way to pan-European strategy, with co-operation between national rail networks necessary to tap international long-distance markets which will become increasingly preponderant as 1993 approaches and the Euro-frontiers come down. The final gel came with the presentation of a study by Euro-consultants A. T. Kearney and Logitech in late 1989. The study showed that on 30 strategic European traffic axes, intermodal rail traffic was a paltry 6.3 million tonnes per year against road's 75 million tonnes. The report went on to identify improvements to be made to intermodal operations which would allow rail to triple carryings by 2005.

Early 1990 saw much excitement around the Euromodal '90 conference in Brussels where all European rail authorities committed themselves to this aim. France and SNCF finds itself at the heart of this process, geographically, as many of the strategic international routes cross France, and managerially, as SNCF freight director, Alain Poinssot, heads an UIC (International Union of Railways) intermodal group whose aim is to organise an international 'Community of Combined Transport Interests'.

SNCF's own contributions to intermodal success have been considerable. In June 1987, the first freight train to operate at 160km/h (100mph) was introduced between Lille and Marseille, conveying principally

Left: **International and transit freight is an important source of revenue for SNCF. In June 1990, Nos BB 8233 and BB 8220 pass through Beziers on a train of VAG group vans carrying parts from Germany to the SEAT car factory in Spain.**
Rail Info Collection

swap-body traffic. Its success has been so rapid that a second pair of trains now run on this route. Other routes since introduced at 160km/h include Perpignan to Rungis (the Paris wholesale food market complex).

Operation at 160km/h is not an aim in itself, but is the only possible method of providing evening of Day A/morning of Day B transport between the most distant French conurbations. 160km/h services are marketed under the FRETCHRONO label but this also includes services at 140km/h (87mph) where distances cannot justify the higher maximum. Speed is also a guarantee of high productivity of wagons, locomotives and also train crew. On the Lille-Marseille run, drivers are changed at Dijon. Thus, each crew member covers over 500 freight kilometres in his shift. This can be compared with an average of less than 300km for top link non-TGV drivers even on passenger duties.

Block Trains

Block trains of 1,500 tonnes upwards are well suited to heavy, low-value products such as coal, ore, cereals, petroleum products and steel, and have been net revenue earners for some time. However, coal and coke traffic has declined from 24 to 11 million tonnes a year since 1975 due to the run-down of French mines, the construction of coastal steel plants and the concentration on nuclear power which now produces 80% of French electricity. To compensate, cereal traffic has grown considerably in recent years due to increased production, and investment in rail loading facilities by French co-operatives.

SNCF reckons that block trains will continue to account for around 50% of freight traffic in years to come. Future consolidation will revolve around investment in further terminals where grouping of wagons into block trains can take place and on improving productivity in the use of locomotives and wagons. SNCF divides its block operations into three distinct products:

- *trains entiers programmés* — trains organised at least 15 days in advance
- *trains entiers concertés* — requested the day before operation
- *trains 'spot'* — requested by the client only a few hours before departure

All of these are either complete trains or *rapilèges* — half trains which are combined with another for the trunk haul.

The introduction of over 300 Class BB 26000 *Sybic* electrics over the next five years will contribute significantly to increased productivity by allowing increased train weights, and therefore revenue at the same time as reducing operating costs. Like Deutsche Bundesbahn's Class 120, these 5,600kW dual-voltage (1,500V dc/25kV ac 50Hz) locomotives, with two 2,800kW synchronous traction motors driving two axles each, are conceived as universal locomotives, able to haul a 16-coach (750 tonne) passenger train at 200km/h or a 2,050 tonne freight at 80km/h up a 1/125 incline. Although beset by delivery delays and teething troubles in 1988/89, 30 locomotives came into service in 1990 and a further 40 were due in 1991.

Aside from the marginal increases in train weight permitted by the *Sybics*, SNCF has been working recently on the development of 'ultra-heavy' block trains. Trains of between 2,000 and 3,000 tonnes have been common for some time, but in 1986, trains of 3,600 tonnes carrying maize from the Aquitaine Region to a starch-producing plant 900km away in Lille were introduced. These are double-headed by Class BB 8500 2,940kW electrics, then by dual-voltage Class BB 25500s of similar power. Investment had to be made in reinforcing the current supply south of Paris, but this has been paid back by the productivity gains made possible by combining two trains.

Further increases in tonnage were found to put too much strain on existing wagon couplings, so rather than buying new wagons, the next development was to operate freights with a coupled locomotive pushing from the rear. This was tried first, starting in 1988, with a 3,600 tonne train of ore from Dunkerque docks to a steel plant near Nancy in the east of France, a run of around 500km, which takes about eight hours. This test was unusual in that it involved cabling the rake of wagons throughout in order to control the rear locomotive from the front. The train was powered by a total of three Class BB 16500 2,580kW electrics, which are necessary because of the severe gradients in the Ardennes region. This rather heavy solution is due to give way to radio control of the rear locomotive for one in the centre of the train. Tests were due to be carried out with this technique during late 1991.

Meanwhile the third, and heaviest so far, ultra-heavy service started carrying lime from Caffiers, in the 'Downs' between Calais and Boulogne, to Sollac steelworks in Dunkerque, 60km away. This 5,200 tonne monster comprises 60 wagons and is powered by two BB 66000 1,030kW diesels up front, with a third pushing. At this stage, the rear locomotive has a driver who communicates with the driver of the leading unit by walkie-talkie.

Sectorisation

Although, like many other European railways, SNCF prefers to call this 'management by activity', it boils down to the same ideas that have served British Rail so well in the last decade. SNCF is moving tentatively towards management and accounting by activity, which allows each market sector director to see his business so much more clearly. From this should flow reductions in management and operating costs, plus the chance to make better investment decisions based on reliable statistics.

Freight Director Alain Poinssot will welcome this more than most at SNCF, as analytical accounting will show the real importance of Fret SNCF to the group as a whole. During 1990, Poinssot had to sit back and watch his trains delayed and even cancelled due to lack of traction as historically, freight services have always the lowest priority when motive power is short. Thus, profitable or

SNCF Freight Traffic in 1988			
	Tonnes (million)	Tonne km (billion)	Receipts FF billion
Domestic	88.54	30.27	7.68
Import/Export	43.70	14.75	4.01
Transit	9.16	5.68	1.00
Total:	141.40	50.70	12.69

potentially profitable freights have been held back whilst locomotives were guaranteed for regional passenger trains covering, on average, 28% of their costs. 1990 was a year of traction shortages due to the late delivery of the *Sybics*, and bad traction planning by the *Materiel* department, which like everything else at SNCF is centralised in Paris. Poinssot will be able to take heart at the arrival of *Sybics* in some numbers, but more importantly by decentralisation and new accounting methods to be brought in during early 1991. Allied to this will be the first 'contracts' to be struck up between Fret SNCF and the operating (*Service de Transport*) and traction (*Service du Matériel*) departments. *Une veritable révolution!*

In its latest five-year plan, SNCF places emphasis on developing international freight traffic. Exchange of goods between EC member countries is constantly increasing and prospects for those countries outside the Community are also encouraging. Norway and Sweden have bought heavily into French industry in order not to be excluded from the EC, and exchanges are on the increase. With the dramatic lifting of the 'Iron Curtain', the potential for exchanges with Eastern Europe is better than ever before. Industry restructuring within Europe is likely to create long distance flows which are ideally suited to rail. Already the Volkswagen group has trains of parts running from German plants to its Spanish subsidiary Seat, a transit of over 1,100km through France.

SNCF aims to consolidate and improve its position in international traffic and hopes to improve its market share from 40 to 45% in the next five years. Intermodal trains will figure prominently in this strategy. For conventional freight, SNCF has worked with other national operators to introduce common tariffs and simplified documentation using information technology to the full. A number of direct international routes have been developed and receive high profile marketing. These include 'Interdelta' which runs from Lyon to Brussels, but whose French catchment includes the whole of the Provence and Rhône-Alpes Regions. The Belgian catchment area covers the important ports of Antwerp, Gent and Zeebrugge. Other direct routes are shown on the map on page 40.

The greatest European opportunity is from the opening of the Channel Tunnel in 1993. The elimination of the two costly and time-consuming breaks of journey which the Channel presently imposes on rail will revolutionise prospects for through trains between France and Britain. Cross-channel freight traffic suitable for rail haulage was around 30 million tonnes in 1988. This traffic has recently been increasing by 8% a year and is likely to grow even faster after the full opening up of European markets in 1993. Rail, via Zeebrugge or Dunkerque accounts for around 2 million tonnes (7%) at present. Forecasts predict rail's share rising to 6.1 million tonnes (16-17%) by 1995, and all this will have at least to transit via France. What could be achieved by the end of the century and after will depend largely on the ability of British Rail and SNCF to provide capacity and reliability, and the provision of suitable wagons for use on the stricter gauged British system. The very existence of the tunnel, leading to cheap and reliable through rail hauls will probably lead to industrial co-operation and restructuring, leading to freight hauls unthought of at present, just as reorganisation of the British steel, coal and electricity generation industries led to long hauls within Britain.

Similar benefits will stem from the conversion of Spanish broad gauge track to standard gauge, scheduled for 1997 if finance permits. At present although some through working is made possible by axle or bogie changes, most freight between the Iberian peninsula and France fights shy of this complication.

Above left: **Although beset by initial teething problems, which delayed their introduction until 1990, the Class 26000 *Sybic* electric locomotives are designed to operate both passenger and freight services. No 26039, shortly after its introduction to service in June 1991, passes Biache St Vaast with the Lille-Marseille 160km/h *FretChrono* service.** *Rail Info Collection*

Left: **Future traffic for the Channel Tunnel includes these Polybulk wagons carrying China Clay between St Austell and Switzerland. Here they are shunted by a 1946-vintage American-built A1A-A1A No 62016 at Dunkerque Ouest in March 1989.** *Rail Info Collection*

As a 'listening railway', SNCF has increasingly found that customers nowadays expect more than the simple supply of a rail trunk haul from A to B. More and more, the possiblity of offering a complete logistical package is extremely important. With its whole or partly-owned subsidiaries in road haulage and container/intermodal transport, SNCF was already well placed. Current moves are to offer warehousing in strategic locations, not only for immediately before or after the rail haul, but also over longer periods where consumer demand makes buffer stocks necessary. A typical example is in white goods such as washing machines and fridges. SNCF, which is strongly positioned on imports of these goods from Italy, found that it might lose out to road if stockage facilities could not be offered. Slowly but surely, what were under-used plots of railway land or buildings found new uses, and rail's markets were retained or expanded. In some deliberately unpublicised cases, space was let out temporarily to road hauliers with no interest in the rail side. As the French say, money has no smell — every penny in the coffers helps.

SNCF has always played a large part in the operations of Garonor, a logistical and warehousing complex near Paris Roissy airport. More recently, the *Société Nationale* took advantage of the closure of its parts store for Hellemmes (Lille) locomotive works to convert the building for use as intermediate warehousing for road hauliers using rail for part of their hauls. *Garolille* is now almost fully utilised and other planned 'logistical platforms' include *Parisud*, unsurprisingly to the south of Paris. In 1989, SNCF increased its warehousing from 110,000 to 200,000m sq, and intends to continue expanding in the near future.

Firms within a Firm

A recent SNCF initiative has been to target niche markets within freight as a whole, which it then serves with a self-contained management unit offering what often looks like a self-contained product, but which uses a rail trunk haul and often road collection/delivery by one of the SNCF road haulage subsidiaries. SNCF believe that the secret of success is to create a small, highly motivated, management team with its own 'bottom line' and as much autonomy as possible in areas of management, marketing and operation.

The first in 1988 was 'Chronofroid' which, as its name suggests, is a high-speed service for chilled and frozen food, which uses 144 refrigerated swap-bodies carried on the FRETCHRONO 140km/h and 160km/h network and a total of 132 lorry trailers for road collection and delivery. The first service was introduced in 1988 between Valenton (Paris) and Avignon, and was a resounding success from the beginning. An Avignon-Lille service was added in 1989, followed by Lyon-Lille, Avignon-Nancy and a second Avignon-Paris in 1990. 'Chronofroid' swap bodies should be running on the Toulouse-Paris, Perpignan-Lille, and Perpignan-Nancy routes in 1991 and between Avignon and Le Mans in 1992. Turnover in 1989 was FF 36 million, with FF 64 million forecast in 1990. A typical 'Chronofroid' customer is Chambourcy, manufacturer of yoghurts and other dairy products, where transport represents 15-20% of turnover. Chambourcy's distribution function is always looking to reduce stocks, and had always used road transport in the past. The competitive price, high capacity of swap bodies and above all, speed of delivery brought by 'Chronofroid', brought a swift transfer to rail.

An area which has exercised the collective minds of SNCF managers for some time is the increasing tendency of retailing and manufacturing to use 'just in time' methods, in which stocks are reduced to an absolute minimum. In general, this has meant going for frequent small shipments rather than less frequent large shipments — a trend which operates directly against rail's natural advantages, where even the wagonload becomes too big a traffic unit. SNCF's first response to this challenge came in early 1990, with the introduction of a first 'Chronodis' service between the Paris area and the Rhône delta (Marseille, Avignon Regions). This is a door-to-door service for palletised goods, using high capacity 'Tautliner' trailers for collection and delivery, with overnight trunk haul at 120km/h in each direction beween Avignon and Villeneuve St Georges. Intermediate warehousing is not systematic, but can be organised where customers need buffer stocks, for example.

Above right: **A classic block train passes through the suburbs of Lille. In this example a Class BB 12000 electric locomotive hauls a rake of empty iron ore wagons towards Dunkerque in September 1986.** *Rail Info Collection*

Right: **'Chronofroid' was the brand name launched in 1988 for a fast service for chilled and frozen foods using refrigerated swap-bodies carried on 'multi-fret' wagons capable of travelling at 160km/h. This train is seen between Valenton (Paris) and Avignon in 1989.** *Rail Info Collection*

The Human Factor

LILLE-FIVES DEPOT – ROUTE KNOWLEDGE TOP LINK DRIVERS

A rail system is, of course, the sum of the many people who work every day to run and maintain it. SNCF employed a total of 206,444 people in 1989, down considerably from the 251,000 working only five years before. This shake out has been one of the principal reasons for the recent financial turnround achieved by the Société Nationale. Staff have been lost from all sectors of railway activity, mainly through natural wastage, but the most visible reductions have been in station staff. Many small stations with no freight activity and very low passenger revenue have seen their booking clerk replaced by an ADDAMS automatic ticket issuing machine (no change given) or their full-time clerk reduced to very limited part-time working at times when trains serve the station. In some cases, the limited service offered by an ADDAMS machine has been supplemented by a weekly long-distance ticket issuing session in the local town hall by a member of SNCF sales staff from the nearest major station. This may seem very surprising to British eyes, but in a country still clinging to village life, the move makes sound commercial sense.

Another source of savings has been in 'bustitution' — this has the long-term effect of removing drivers and guards from the SNCF balance sheet, although perhaps adding new employment to the separate accounts of SCETA, SNCF's 83% owned road transport subsidiary. Station staff may also be saved, but in some cases remain to deal with freight traffic and to issue passenger tickets — SNCF has not yet perfected on-bus issue of long distance bus/rail tickets. Rolling stock maintenance depot and workshop closures are also a visible sign of belt-tightening, although made possible by the reduced maintenance needs of modern rolling stock. In the past five years, Le Mans, La Rochelle, Nîmes, Lyon Mouche and Paris La Plaine depots have all lost allocations, whilst in the near future Thionville will go, with Mohon likely to follow.

Whilst many railway jobs will always be carried out behind the scenes, that of driver is necessarily at the forefront of everyday operation. SNCF drivers work to conditions which are considerably different from those on BR. In many ways they are more skilled and their everyday job can be considered as more difficult. As a general rule, they are better paid than their British counterparts, with retirement at the amazingly early age of 50, which makes for a much younger profession than in the UK.

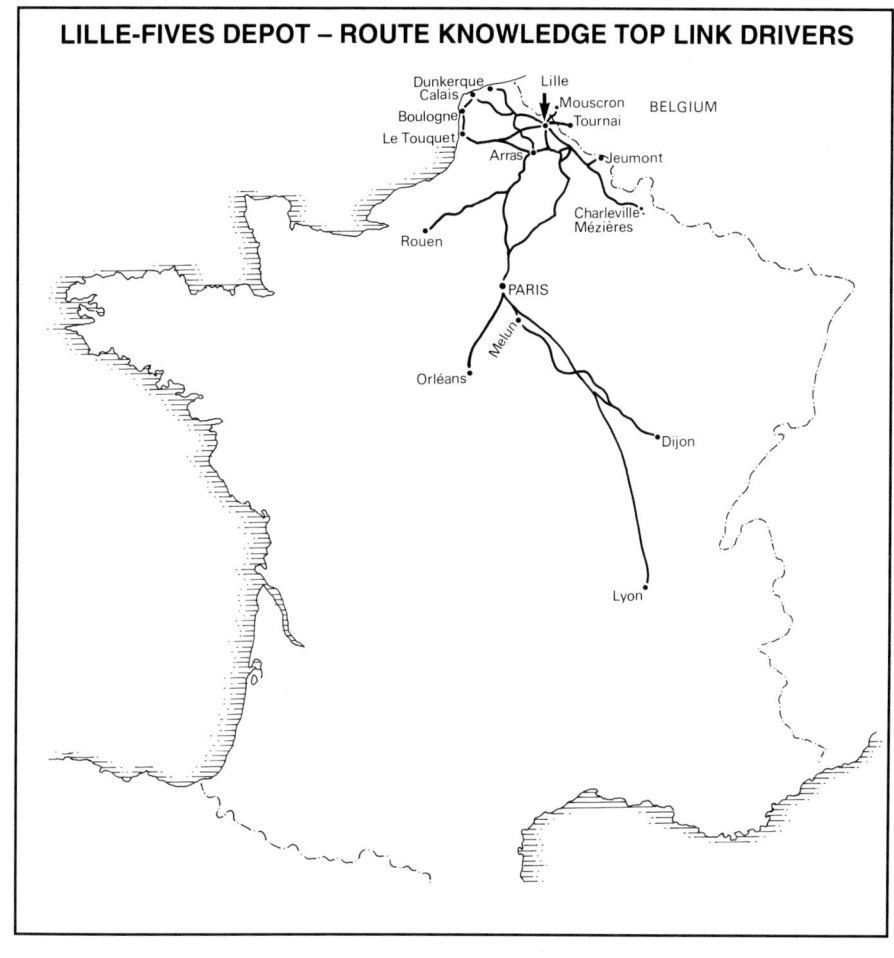

SNCF drivers are recruited at three different levels. The most poorly qualified are 19/20-year-olds who join SNCF after (for men) their military service, and who have left school at 16-18 with rather poor results in subjects leaning to the technical. Candidates are subjected to two days of tests of intellectual and physical aspects plus an interview covering amongst other things, the candidate's motiviation. Those selected become *conducteurs de manoeuvres* — shunting drivers, and follow a 4-6 month training course covering driving and motive power maintenance theory, during which they start to drive lowly forms of traction over short distances.

After passing an exam including written, oral and practical tests, the apprentice becomes an *élève-conducteur* or student driver. It is at this level that candidates having the *baccalauréat* (equivalent to A-Levels) enter the profession after entrance tests but without passing through the phase of shunting driver. The student driver now enters his main period of training which takes 10-12 months, during which he learns the rule book and technical details of at least one diesel and one electric locomotive class. Individual work at this stage is severely marked. Any drop below 60% is followed by a warning and if a second warning follows, the student driver is out! He continues to drive trains such as trip freights over short distances during this time.

It should be noted that SNCF drivers are trained to drive trains with the minimum energy and brake material required and are aided by guides for each train which give the exact speed

45

Left: **One aspect of staff reductions over recent years has been the closure of maintenance depots. Lyon Mouche, Nîmes and Paris La Plaine are recent closures whilst Mohon, Les Aubrais (Orleans), Paris La Chapelle and Thionville are due to close soon. Here diesel No 68061 is seen under heavy overhaul at Chalindrey depot during 1991.** *Rail Info Collection*

Below left: **A TGV driver at the controls of one of the TGV-Sud-Est rakes. TGVs are equipped with a number of safety devices. The wheel, directly in front of the driver, is the main power controller which incorporates a vigilance device. The driver must acknowledge each signal aspect with this or with a floor pedal. Also visible are the radio telephones, which are used to communicate with the main Paris Control Centre. TGV sets are normally single-manned despite the distances driven. Fives driverswork Lille-Lyon trains (700km) is around 4hr 40min without a break. Sud Est region drivers work Paris-Nice trains, which are non-stop, for 5hr 15min to Toulon - a distance of 845km.** *SNCF*

necessary to keep time and the sections when the driver can allow the train to coast. Although drivers are paid a bonus for time recovered on late running trains, and must record the exact reason for every delay, speeding is a disciplinary matter and can be detected by analysis of the locomotive's 'black box'. This also records the aspect of every signal passed and is invaluable when accidents occur.

At the end of the student driver's course, there is an extensive exam which passes him to drive any train up to 120km/h over whatever area is covered by his route knowledge. A whole day of written exams covers rules and regulations, train documentation and reactions to a host of theoretical incidents. A second day is devoted to oral tests then two more days are spent driving with a *Chef de Traction* (CDT) on hand. Usually, a range of normal service trains including local passenger and freight is covered, during which the CDT will continue questioning and simulate minor breakdowns which the driver must be able to rectify.

From this point on, there are no more exams, and the driver's career progresses according to his aptitude and experience. At the beginning, he will not be incorporated into a regular rota of duties but instead will be at the disposal of the depot for the replacement of absent colleagues and driving conditional services. In most cases, the driver will not know what duties he is to work until a day or two beforehand. Depending on local conditions, this period of a driver's career may last anything from two to eight years. As is the case in London, drivers tend to be in shortest supply in the Paris region and therefore climb the ladder much more quickly there. After this period, and on the recommendation of the *Chef de Traction* supervising him, the driver will be passed for 140km/h and promoted to *conducteur de route* — main line driver. In general, he will now know further in advance what duties he will be working but he may not yet be on a regular rota. A further entrance level is that of candidates with the *baccalauréat* and two years of studies. These people are admitted with much reduced entrance tests, and receive accelerated training as student drivers which bring them up to main line driver standard much more quickly.

After a minimum of 12 years, total service, it is almost automatic for a driver to become *conducteur de route principal* — senior main line driver, and be passed for 160km/h trains. Within this grade, which is the most senior, he can go one step higher by applying to drive the fastest trains — 200km/h Corail passenger rakes and TGVs up to 300km/h. No extra basic pay is received for higher speeds, but bonuses for distance travelled are bound to rise.

The *Chef de Traction* or traction inspector is a supervisory post with responsibility for training, assessing and finally promoting drivers. In general, they are recruited from the most experienced senior main line drivers and are responsible for keeping track of 20-35 drivers each. Their duties consist mainly of riding beside 'their' drivers, bringing them up to date on rule changes and continually testing their traction, rule book and route knowledge. When necessary, they are also responsible for disciplinary measures. As they are in constant contact with the drivers, they are in a position to decide who is suitable for promotion. In the case of Lille Fives depot, there are 15 CDTs for 220 drivers, as certain CDTs are in charge of a few drivers but have greater responsibility for overall training. Immediately above the CDTs is the depot manager responsible for drivers and guards — the *Chef de Dépôt de Ligne*. He is the final arbiter in matters of promotion and is generally promoted from the CDTs themselves.

In principle, an SNCF driver works a 39hr week, which works out at a 7hr 48min day. The famous concept of 'flexible rostering' means that within this average the duty length can vary — SNCF permit a maximum of 11 hours for daytime, with a break after six hours, or eight hours for night duties. One important factor in driving long distances is that SNCF drivers sleep away from home about one night in two. These rest periods are normally a minimum of nine hours, whilst rest periods at home, of which there are around 112 per year, are always 14 hours or more. Drivers accept this as part of their work but conditions in the *foyers* where the men sleep were one of the biggest complaints during the long winter strike in 1985/86. Although it is logical that Lille drivers sleep out at Paris, Dijon or Rouen, it seems strange that rota planners force them to bed down at Lens (36km from home) Valenciennes (48km), Hazebrouck (46km) or Somain (48km). It would be interesting to know whether the cost of providing accommodation and 'sleeping out' bonuses, plus the social cost to drivers' families really outweighs the operating convenience gained.

In order to see how this works in practice, I analysed the duties from Fives depot in Lille. Fives is principally a passenger depot, freight duties being worked from La Délivrance depot at the marshalling yard across the city. Unsurprisingly, Fives drivers cover all lines emanating from Lille, that is to Calais, Boulogne, Dunkerque, Tourcoing, Tournai (just inside Belgium) and Paris via Amiens. Drivers with more experience also reach Rouen via Amiens and Charleville-Mézières, on the line to Strasbourg, plus the Lille-Paris diversionary route via St Quentin.

On freight work, Fives men cover the *Grande Ceinture* freight line around Paris to a variety of yards as far as Juvisy on the Paris Austerlitz-Bordeaux line. What is perhaps more surprising is the range of top link drivers who operate considerably beyond Paris. Drivers on rota 120, for instance, drive TGVs direct from Lille to Lyon, a distance of approximately 430 miles, further than Euston-Glasgow. The same drivers reach Dijon Ville daily when they take the 100mph Lille-Marseille freight on to the Sud-Est region, and with certain summer-dated night passenger trains. One freight per day also brings Fives drivers as far as Les Aubrais (Orléans) on the Atlantique region. This is in order to keep route knowledge fresh during winter — during the summer timetable, certain summer-dated trains go through from Lille to the southwest particularly trains of pilgrims to Lourdes. Total route knowledge is an amazing 2,300km — about 1,400 miles (see map). In order to reach a similar total, a York driver would have to know all local routes plus King's Cross-Aberdeen, Edinburgh-Glasgow Queen Street, York-Liverpool via Leeds, York-Birmingham-Bristol, the whole of the North London line and more. This may seem excessive and, indeed, some drivers complain that keeping this knowledge, plus that of up to 15 types of traction, is too much to ask.

Over the page is an extract covering the first three weeks of top link rota 120 at Fives. During this period the driver sleeps out six times, mainly at Paris Charolais — the period analysed covers the winter sports season, which sees increased TGV services between Lille and the Alps. The longest duties are those covering 1,130km (702 miles) in a 10-11 hour duty. In duty 047, the driver signs on at 13.18, takes his TGV ecs into Lille station, then departs for Lyon at 14.00, stopping at Douai 14.18/20, Arras 14.35/37, Longueau 15.05/07 and at Valenton near Paris at around 16.25 to couple a second rake from Rouen. There follows a non-stop run over the LGV with arrival at Lyon Part Dieu at 18.31 and Perrache at 18.41. Our driver then takes a well earned, unpaid break of approximately one hour. He then takes TGV 688 from Perrache at 20.13 calling at Part Dieu then non-stop to Paris Gare de Lyon arriving at 22.27. He then walks to the adjacent depot at Charolais, signs off at 22.59 and sleeps in the *foyer* there. If we can imagine high-speed lines criss-crossing the UK, this duty is the approximate equivalent of driving King's Cross-Dundee then back to York in one shift. In general, long duties like 047 are followed by a shorter day of lighter work. In the case of duty 051, he regains Lille by riding the RER across Paris then working the 14.12 Paris-Lille the 251km back to base.

Several points are worth noting in this short extract. Firstly, the quantity of work on TGVs through to the Sud-Est region. Altogether four of the 14 duties here involve TGVs between Lille and Lyon. Sunday duty 107 sees the driver riding on the cushions Lille-Paris, then working a return Gare de Lyon-Lyon Perrache TGV with 15 minutes turnround at

Above right: **Lille drivers regularly drive TGVs plus three different types of electric locomotives, including Class BB 22200 which are based far away at Dijon and Marseille. Drivers may also be called on to drive up to 10 other types of traction. Here No BB 22224 enters Douai with the evening Tourcoing-Paris Trans-Europe-Express now downgraded to 'Rapide' status.** *Rail Info Collection*

Right: **The 'longest day' for the drivers of Lille Fives depot is a diagram which sees them working on a Lille-Lyon TGV service followed by a Lyon-Paris working. Here TGV rake No 39 is seen at Seclin soon after departure from Lille.** *Rail Info Collection*

EXTRACT FROM LILLE FIVES DEPOT ROTA 120
(Winter Service 15/02/91-11/03/91)

	Duty No	Sign On At	Sign Off At	Duty Length hr min	Revenue Driving hr min	Stock§ Movement hr min	Unpaid Break hr min	On Cushions hr min	km*
Monday	Rest Day								
Tuesday	Rest Day								
Wednesday	080	13.35 Fives	21.30 Paris C	7.55	3.07	4.33	—	0.15	277
Thursday	090	10.20 Paris C	20.20 Fives	10.00	6.46	1.39	1.35	—	1,130
Friday	060	17.12 Fives	00.48 Dijon	7.36	4.58	2.38	—	—	603
Saturday	076	11.20 Dijon	20.24 Fives	9.04	2.17	3.17	1.30	2.00	251
Sunday	047	13.18 Fives	22.59 Paris C	9.41	6.55	1.38	1.08	—	1,130
Monday	051	11.13 Paris C	17.30 Fives	6.17	2.14	3.43	—	0.20	251
Tuesday	Rest Day								
Wednesday	Rest Day								
Thursday	010	14.49 Fives	21.49 Fives	7.00	4.31	2.29	—	—	502
Friday	085	14.59 Fives	21.30 Paris C	6.31	2.54	3.17	—	0.20	277
Saturday	096	09.24 Paris C	20.20 Fives	10.56	6.37	2.01	2.11	0.07	1,130
Sunday	107	13.35 Fives	00.29 Paris C	10.54	4.44	1.54	1.24	2.52	864
Monday	111	11.00 Paris C	14.49 Fives	3.49	—	—	—	3.49	0
Tuesday	Rest Day								
Wednesday	Rest Day								
Thursday	080	13.35 Fives	21.30 Paris C	7.55	3.07	4.33	—	0.15	277
Friday	095	09.24 Paris C	20.20 Fives	10.56	6.37	1.43	2.29	0.07	1,130
Saturday	036	12.17 Fives	18.41 Fives	6.24	1.55	3.01	—	1.28	153
Sunday	Rest Day								
Monday	Rest Day								

Paris C = Paris Charolais (Gare de Lyon)
§ Includes empty stock and light engine movements, plus signing on, walking and locomotive preparation and inspection.
* Revenue earning kilometres only.

FIVES DEPOT ROTA
(27 January – 20 April 1991)

Week	Monday	Tuesday	Wednesday	Thursday	Friday	Saturday	Sunday
01	RP	RP	080	090	060	076	047
02	051	RP	RP	010	085	096	107
03	111	RP	RP	080	095	036	RP
04	RP	010	020	X030	040	056	RP
05	RP	D	100	110	105	115	RP
06	040	050	RP	RP	025	086	097
07	010	060	070	RP	RP	126	127
08	080	090	060	070	RP	RP	017
09	060	070	010	020	X030	RP	RP
10	121	100	110	RP	RP	040	057
11	101	110	RP	RP	010	016	087
12	090	020	X030	RP	RP	106	117
13	131	RP	RP	040	055	D	RP
14	RP	040	050	100	110	RP	RP
15	020	X030	040	050	125	RP	RP
16	RP	080	090	060	075	026	037

AMP: 07.45 ——— Average Duty Length 7h45 min
EFF: 07.03 ——— Average Paid Time 7h03 min
KMS: 509.9 ——— Average Duty Kms 509.9
RP: 110.5 par an ——— Rest Period 110.5 per year

Perrache! In return, Paris Lyon men work Lyon-Lille TGVs, all of which shows the complete flexibility that SNCF drivers show over the territory they work in. Although the quantity of work away from home may seem surprising, work over the Sud-Est LGV by Lille drivers is an essential precursor to the opening of the Channel Tunnel and the TGV-Nord line. From June 1993, Lille will become a major interchange for British and Belgian passengers travelling to the south of France, and up to 10 trains a day will work through to the Sud-Est.

From the analysis, it may also seem that drivers spend a great deal of time on stock movement. However, within this time is included the 10 minutes signing on/off time plus time spent preparing the locomotive and in some cases giving it a daily inspection. SNCF drivers are trained to be responsible for the motive power they drive, and to resolve minor breakdowns which occur in service. Any breakdown that is not solved by the driver and which causes a delay to passengers will later be investigated by a *Chef de Traction* to ensure that the driver followed the correct procedure. Given such thorough-going practices it is unsurprising that SNCF services are generally punctual.

What are SNCF drivers paid for this skilful but unsociable job? Starting salary in 1991 for a 'shunting driver' was FF 5,379 a month, whilst bottom whack for a 'senior main line driver' was FF 7,283. Taking the '13th month' bonus into account, these translate as around £7,000-£9,500 per year. However, a senior driver with 15 years' experience would probably earn nearer FF 10,000 basic per month to which must be added a host of bonuses. These include one linked to the number of kilometres driven, the rate varying with the type of train, plus other bonuses for night driving, one-man work, sleeping away from home, Sunday work and, most interestingly, one for time made up on late running trains. The aggregate of these bonuses often approaches 40-50% of the basic rate, which for the aforementioned senior driver could bring his gross pay up to FF 14,000 per month or around £17,000 per year. When judging his pay, it must be remembered that SNCF drivers are not permitted to work overtime so this salary is regular but also final.